No Two People See the Same Rainbow

No Two People See the Same Rainbow

THE NEW METHOD TO UNDERSTAND THE REAL YOU, PLUS THE FREEDOM AND POWER TO CHANGE WHAT YOU DON'T LIKE

BY

BILL TRUBY
JOANN TRUBY

EDITED BY W. A. NEWMAN

TRUBY ACHIEVEMENT CENTER
MOUNT SHASTA, CALIFORNIA

No Two People See the Same Rainbow
Bill & Joann Truby

Published by Angel's Dream Publishing Company
P.O. Box 1440
Mt. Shasta, California 96067
Tel; Fax; Pager: 877-377-3279

Find us on the World Wide Web at: www.trubyachievementcenter.com

Cover design: Marie Wells, Marie-Josee Studio
Interior design and illustrations: William A. Newman and
Wordsmiths Marketing

Colophon
This book was created with Adobe InDesign 2.0 on a Macintosh G3. The fonts used are Adobe Garamond, Gazelle and Copperplate Gothic.

ISBN 0-9725897-4-0
Printed and bound in the United States of America by LSI

Dedication

To each and every person who has participated in our
Personal Growth Intensive.

May this book be a reflection of your experience,
and inspiration for your continued growth.

Bill and Joann

Table of Contents

Introduction

It is after dark. The outside lights illuminate the snow that gently falls on an already existing blanket of white, perfectly setting the mood for reflection. Five people sit in our living room feeling very much at home, comfortably watching the fire, waiting for the first step in this journey called the Personal Growth Intensive – "PGI" for those more intimate with the experience.

This is the winter setting for the seminar we enjoy giving so much. Other months provide a variety of backdrops for this time of intense, personal exploration and growth. But it doesn't really matter what it's like outside. Each season is just a different backdrop for the main event. And that event is a life-changing experience, the Personal Growth Intensive (PGI).

We designed the PGI from both of our perspectives. As we tell you about these perspectives, let us introduce you to the writing style of this book. For the most part we will be writing together. When one of us has something to say from our individual experience or perspective, we will introduce it by using our name. When we return to writing together, we will return to using the terms "our" or "we." The next few paragraphs will illustrate this.

I, Bill, am a licensed marriage and family therapist with a master's degree in psychology. I do not currently have a private practice. Our life of travel, writing and speaking along with our training and consulting company (The Truby Achievement Center) keeps us too busy for me to carry on a private practice.

I have always been interested in the sciences, both the natural sciences and the science of human behavior. I come at this book from this perspective. In chapter four I will tell you how the core model used in our PGI and in this book was created. For now I will tell you that my highest joy is making a positive difference in people's life. The concepts, principles and models in this book powerfully help do just that.

I, Joann, have the same "greatest joy" as Bill. It gives me deep fulfillment and intense pleasure to watch someone find fulfillment and growth. I come to this writing with the perspective of over 25 years of working with individual's and groups, coaching, mentoring and teaching. No matter what role I have been in, my core activity was to take an individual from where they were to where they wanted to be.

I believe in people. When I am working with a person I use an intuitive approach to help that person find the internal and external strengths that can provide success and growth. I like being positive, thinking positive and helping those whom I work with be grounded in the strength of not only positive thinking but having faith to face the most difficult situations and know there will be a positive outcome.

From our similar desires and complimentary perspectives, we designed the PGI. It is a three day event where we only allow five people to come at a time. The PGI helps people fully understand who they are, what may be blocking them from continued growth, how to completely cleanse of those blocks as well as old baggage, then implement tools and methodologies for continued growth. Without fail, people report gaining a sense of peace and freedom as well as a confident personal power as a result of the PGI.

The man from Colorado who had been in therapy for 14 years, the man from California who was aware of a personal problem he didn't know how to deal with for 21 years, the woman from Wisconsin who continually lived a life of bondage and fear, the woman from Illinois who felt successful but unhappy, and more – all went through the PGI and found...themselves. They understood who the ***real*** person was inside and how to live a life that was free. They learned how to live that life on purpose, and with purpose.

In this book you will hear their stories. You will also learn about the principles behind the method we are inferring to here. We know it works. We have seen it work in hundreds of lives. But it's not magic (though it feels like it sometimes). It is simply a clear understanding of cause and effect then changing the cause to have a different effect. The principles in this book are simple yet powerful, easy to understand yet complex enough to fuel hours of conversation.

We want you to understand, too, that this book does not go to the depth of an actual Personal Growth Intensive seminar. Our book is designed to teach you the basic content and process. We know it will be helpful but when you read it, you will not have the benefit of a facilitated group process. If you find difficulty in grasping or implementing some of the concepts or tools, you may want to get help from a friend, a minister or a counselor. Ask them to read the portion you are struggling with and assist you as you work with it.

A comment about where the content of this book came from: It would be impossible to list the multitude of sources that contributed to the writing of this book. The principles, concepts and methodologies all come from years of eclectic exposure to various human and spiritual disciplines as well as overt study of the sciences of physics, quantum physics, health and nutrition, psychology, systems theory and more. Personal experience and experiment also played a major role in creating the theories in this book as well as determining which tools were useful or not.

Let us give you some suggestions about how to read this book. These suggestions were inspired when one of our friends, Joy Taylor, read the book and told us this:

"If you read this book correctly it can change your life. It is not just another mental exercise to file in your brain to use as an analytical reference. It is an experiential opportunity. It needs to be read with compassion. It needs to be read to the hurt places, the wounded places, within you.

The book is a conversational book – you, Bill & Joann, conversing with the reader, and the reader having an internal conversation with self. Each time, when I read your manuscript, I found some quite time, did what you asked me to in the book, and found that it was a great growth experience for me!"

Our suggestions, then, are these: Be honest and open with yourself as you read the book. Take the time to do the exercises *before* you move on to the next section or chapter. And, if you must, read the book through quickly to get the concepts, then return to each principle or teaching, look at yourself clearly in the context of each principle, then apply the learning.

If you follow these suggestions you will undoubtedly reap the benefits others have by going through the process. So let's get started. We can't wait for you to find what you are looking for. And when you do, we'd like to hear your story. Use the contact information at the end of this book and tell us about you. We'd love to hear how your rainbow shines.

Chapter 1

YOUR PERSONAL RAINBOW... ...WHO ARE YOU?

Who are you…really? When you turn off the television, turn off the radio, the computer, the walkman, the phone, and you are left with just you, what is left? Who is left? Who are you? *How* are you?

Imagine yourself alone, in the privacy of just being you, totally honest with yourself, willing to take a scrutinizing look at the real you, the you deep inside, the you that drives your decisions, guides your thoughts and delivers your perspective on the moment. When you are in this moment of ultimate reality, under the light of honest scrutiny, what goes on inside your mind? What questions come to you? Are you able to truly see and understand "you" or are you so busy living life with, or for, other people that you still don't even know yourself?

What fears haunt you? What insecurities? Are you lonely? Are you wanting? What needs are going unfulfilled? What hurts or jealousies do you carry around as baggage? How weighted down are you? What are you missing? Are you confident in yourself and your life? Are you able to be honest enough with yourself to answer these questions?

It is a rather rare moment for most people to put the statue of self on display, then walk around it viewing every aspect of their being. And the reason for the rarity is because most people get an inkling of some aspect of themselves they don't understand or don't like, but they don't know how to deal with it. So, instead, they get immersed in the inertia of life, busily living out the expectations of others or the hand-me-down script from the past.

It's safer that way. What you don't face, you don't have to deal with. And, what you don't face that you don't know how to deal with (which is more often the case) seemingly frees you from having do anything about these fears and insecurities. The problem, though, is they still seep out in life and relationships causing glitches, conflict, sadness, even boredom.

So, what people see and what we portray, even to ourselves, is something different than what is going on deep in the reality of our true self. And that is a fearful, stressful and insecure way to live life.

Oh sure, we can cover it up fine. We have the right answers, we say and do the right things. But remember, this is about standing in the light of honest scrutiny, looking at our real self, the one we are barely conscious of, the one that is standing inside the closet of our soul, door cracked, peeking out, knowing what we are really like but not possessing the nerve to step into the light of day.

Janet is a perfect example of this. She attended one of our Personal Growth Intensives (PGI). This is a three-day seminar where only five people at a time attend. During this seminar, the process of learning takes people through the essence of what you will learn in this book. But the PGI entails more expansive exercises and interactions as well as individual and personal attention.

Janet was married to a prominent professional in the community (and of course, her name has been changed as has everyone else whom we refer to in this book). Seems like everyone in town knew her and her husband. She epitomized what many women wanted to be and wanted to have. She was beautiful; she had an adoring husband, and she could claim a successful profession in the medical field. It looked as though she had it all together. In fact, when you talked to anyone about Janet they seemed to glow with love for her.

Janet oozed happiness and love. She had a lot of personal power yet could be soft and compassionate enough to sooth her most troubled friend. She truly had it all together, from her beauty to her marriage to her profession to her much-coveted house to her multitude of friends to her wardrobe that never seemed to have a repeat performance. She exemplified happiness and the perfect life. But was that really what was going on? Hardly.

As Janet began to be honest with herself and the other participants at the PGI she and we realized that her life was not all it was cracked up to be. She was chronically sad, disappointed in her life and marriage, lonely and without hope. Her way of coping was to believe that someday, when this life was over, Heaven would make up for all she was now missing.

But it was a struggle and a burden for Janet to live life the way she was living it, carrying all the sadness, loneliness, fears and emptiness inside while living the perfect life, for everyone else we might add, on the outside. The amount of energy to expend to do this during her nearly fifty years of life, her twenty-some year marriage and her constant role model standing in the community was phenomenal. Even she didn't know how she kept it up.

Janet is an example of the two parts we see in most people. The outside "mask" with its accompanying portrayal and interaction, and the inside true self, which affects our emotional, psychological and relational well-being.

The good news is this, however: Janet is an example of what *can* happen in your life. After learning the concepts in the PGI and in this book, she became happy and fulfilled and was able to live life with such freedom that even those who thought she was perfect saw a difference in her. She radiated a lighter spirit and even more confidence and a happiness that went beyond her previous display of togetherness. Her husband noticed the difference, and they were able to have a richer, fuller, more meaningful relationship because of Janet's growth.

And we'll show you how to have this kind of result in your life too. The concepts in this book have been proven to be successful for the past twenty years of our experience in teaching them. They will help you too.

We've seen so many people like Janet but with different manifestations of the incongruence between the inner and outer self. There was John who constantly lived in fear. It wasn't obvious to others. What was obvious, though, was John's inconsistency, his procrastination, his lack of follow through, his ineffective people skills. All of these were coming from his inner self that was so afraid of failure. He wanted to please everyone. He would say what each person wanted to hear when he was with them but would frequently be caught saying something different to someone else.

John found the principles in this book to be what he was looking for to be free of his people-pleasing life. He was able to get rid of old hurts. He was able to understand why he did what he did. And in the finding, he also found the solutions resulting in his ability to live life, like Janet, freely, happy and with more meaningful relationships.

Janet was living a burdensome perfect life and John was living a burdensome subservient life. Betty is another example of someone who was living with an invisible life. Growing up in a big family she found herself playing many roles in that family. She was a "parent" to her two younger siblings, a "wife" to her father who sought her confidence all the time, even complaining to Betty about her mother (his real wife). She was a "daughter" to her grandparents spending more time with them, her grandfather specifically, than her real parents.

Betty was so busy living out these roles that she didn't have any friends her age while growing up. Further, in adulthood, because she didn't know any better, she married a man to whom she related more as a mother than a wife. And in her professional life as well as her personal life she found herself simply living out the roles of her past rather than being who she wanted to be.

Betty had no clue about who *she* was, but she, too, found freedom and happiness through the concepts in this book. Further, she was able to explore and find who she really was and live out her *self* rather than living out the self her enmeshed family demanded she be. Her words about her growth and freedom were these:

It was great being with you at the PGI. I feel GREAT! My husband and I are happier than we have been in a long time. Also, nothing seems to bother me. My friends whom I talk to on the phone cannot believe the difference in my voice. They say they can tell that I am much happier…"

We will show you how to have these results too.

So here we have Janet, John and Betty, all three professionals with graduate degrees, well paid, and working successfully in high-level positions in each of their organizations. Each had what many people think is necessary for happiness and well-being. But their beings weren't very well at all. What happened? What caused this?

Typically, most people don't wake up one morning and decide to have the sorrows, fears, hurts and wants that exist in their life. Instead, these *result* from experiences, events and relationships from the past. Something happens, we learn a concept or a conditioned response, and we carry that forward into the living of our life. Each episode and learning cumulates with what else we have learned and experienced resulting in a composite picture of what we have been. This mosaic, then, becomes the backdrop of our life resulting in our confusing the inertia of our past with the reality of our present. (We will talk more about this in the next chapter).

Evidence of this inertial existence is all around us. Something gets initiated and we carry it forward without future thought but with extended habit. Then, this extended habit becomes unbendable truth or an indisputable fact.

A simple example of this is the concept of the hands of our analogue watches and clocks moving what we know as "clockwise." This circular movement of the hands from left to right has become the *only* acceptable way of making a watch. It is *the* way it *must* be done. In fact, to make the hands of a clock move counter clockwise would not only be counter to what we want, expect and have learned, it would also be "wrong."

Yet the only reason clockwise movement goes from left to right is because watches were invented in the northern hemisphere. The movement of the hands replicated what the inventors were familiar with; the movement of the shadow on a sun dial, which moves circularly, from left to right...or "clockwise." If watches were invented in the southern hemisphere, the shadow moves just the opposite direction. So if that had been the case, counterclockwise movement would have been the standard.

That little piece of trivia has had deep and long lasting effects on how watches are made. To change the movement at this time would be nearly impossible. Yet the movement of the hands was not based on a right or wrong fact, or a good or bad principle; it was based on experience then perpetuated into the inertial habit of that experience.

Our dollar bill is a piece of paper. It has practically no inherent value. Yet that piece of paper has become *very* valuable in our world. You can have the same size piece of paper with a different image and number printed on it and it becomes even more valuable. How did this happen?

The history is simple, really. Gold and silver, which has some inherent value because of its rarity and people's wants, was too hard to carry. Eventually a piece of paper indicating that you had an amount of gold or silver became the valuable document. But it was valuable because there was gold or silver to back it up.

Remember when our paper currency said on it, "This note is *exchangeable* for legal tender for all debts public and private?" Gradually there became more paper than gold or silver thus making it impossible to exchange all the notes in existence for gold or silver (legal tender). Our government then made the paper, the note, the valuable commodity. Now our currency says, "This note *is* legal tender for all debts public and private."

Once again, present day reality is based on a trail of occurrences that were not designed to have the outcome they do; they just do. No one set out to make a piece of paper valuable, it just happened over time. Yet to change it would be very difficult if not impossible.

Every organization or person we have worked with during the past 25 years has virtually all perspectives, attitudes, beliefs and interactions *resulting* from past relationships, events, or experiences. Present tense reality exists from past tense perspective.

Janet, John and Betty all exhibited this fact. They were living out life based on how they *learned to* live it, not on how they *decided* to live it. Each had their unique perspective from their individual past resulting in their varied and unfortunate present. How each person saw life resulted in how each person lived life.

The dynamics of this are very much like looking at a rainbow. Did you know that no two people see the same rainbow? The physics of the situation prevent this.

A rainbow forms when light passes through raindrops that act like a prism separating the white light into the colors of the rainbow. The light passing through the "prism" enters your eyes and presents you with your own personal rainbow.

The reason it is yours and only yours is because of the angles involved. As the light passes through the raindrops, it enters your eyes at a specific angle that cannot be duplicated. A person standing right next to you sees a different rainbow because that person's eyes are receiving the light from a different angle.

But you are both seeing a rainbow, right? Yes, but it is a different rainbow coming from your individual perspectives. And this is just like life.

Three effects are happening here. First, there are the basic physics principles for creating a rainbow. Second, there is the fact that each person is seeing a rainbow. Third, each person is seeing a specific, individual rainbow resulting from the individual perspective.

Life has basic principles that govern it. In fact, there are basic principles that govern *anything and everything* you do. Whether gardening, cooking, canoeing or operating a business, *every* activity or interaction that you undertake has basic principles that determine your level of success depending on how much you understand and give attention to them. It is incredibly important that you understand the principles of aerodynamics if you are going to fly a plane. And it is even more important that you *follow* them if you are going to fly the plane safely.

Though there are basic principles that govern anything we do, there is still much variety, sometimes an infinite amount of variety, you can achieve depending on your creativity or interaction with those principles. One of our sons is a chef. Certainly, he has to give attention to the basic principles of preparing food. But there is an endless amount of ways he can interact with those principles causing creative and delicious outcomes which sets him apart as the excellent chef he is.

I, Bill, have two sisters my father raised in his second marriage. They are younger than I am, of course, but we laughed when we began comparing some of the concepts and behaviors we had individually learned while growing up with the same father. None of us would sneeze or cough into our right hands for example. Why? Dad taught us to cover our mouth during a sneeze or cough with our left hand. That way, when we shook hands with someone (with our right hand) we would not spread any germs.

Further, when reviewing the lives of my two brothers, my two sisters and me, I realized we all were governed by the same basic principles and family dynamics (the basic physics of creating a rainbow). Each of us could talk about the similar experiences and training we had growing up as well as our interactions with the various members of our family (each person seeing a rainbow). Yet each of us has different perspectives on life, different work ethics, different fears and concerns, different strengths and skills; we are each very different people at the core of our being. For example, growing up with the pains and limitation of our existence resulted in different beliefs and behavior because of our different perspectives and personalities. I tried to take the initiative of making everyone okay, while my brother withdrew and stuck his head in the sand like an ostrich (each person seeing their individual rainbow and reacting accordingly).

You see, no two people see the same rainbow, but the rainbow each person sees determines individual perspectives on life and how life is lived. Each person is unique in his or her experience and interaction in life. Even two people who grow up in the same family can have different perspectives, beliefs and reactions. The principles that govern our experience remain constant. Our collective perspective that certain aspects of life exist is usually constant. The specific aspects of *our individual* interaction with the moment of an event or relationship determine *our individual* perspective and reaction.

What you will learn in this book is how to identify your specific "rainbow" or perspective on life. You will learn why you are the way you are, what makes you tick, and understand how you came to be this way. You will understand where your fears and concerns, your strengths and your weaknesses, your insecurities and needs came from and what to do with them.

In short, what you will learn is how to live out a principle of life we deeply believe in. We teach this principle to as many people as we can. We believe this is the way to live life to its fullest in meaningful existence and greatest happiness. The principle we are referring to is this:

Live life freely, on purpose, with purpose.

Here is what we mean. Living life freely means to be free of any baggage you may be carrying. Too many people live life burdened with old hurts, pains, jealousies, angers, and other emotions or memories that continue to affect how they live life today. The experience or relationship that caused this baggage may have been a normal, legitimate occurrence. Someone took advantage of you. You were hurt, violated, wronged. Without dealing with that issue to closure, you carry the emotional results and scars, the memories and the perspectives of that experience or relationship into your present and future.

Further, a lack of living life freely occurs when we have old habits or conditioned responses governing how we live life today. If we are not living life freely, we are *reacting* through life. *Anything* that predetermines how we interact or engage with a person or a situation takes control of us, thus we are not free. On the other hand, living life freely means we have been able to obtain control over our habitual conditioned responses and we have gotten rid of the old baggage we have been carrying.

We will show you how to do this in this book. You will learn how to live life so freely you feel like you are flying, especially if you are one of those people who is extremely weighted and burdened with the life that has been before.

Living life "on purpose" means you are not reactively living life but are proactively doing so. When you are living life freely, you are free to choose. Before, you made automatic responses that governed your behavior and interactions. And when you are free to choose how you live life, how you respond to situations, how you interact with others, you are living life "on purpose."

Living life "with purpose" means you understand *why* you exist, and you stir that into everything you do. You are the happiest and most fulfilled when you understand what your natural talents, characteristics and contributive aspects are, and then are able to live out and amplify those in all you do. That is living life "with purpose."

In this book you will come to fully understand how to live life freely, on purpose, with purpose. We have seen hundreds of people find this kind of existence always with incredible outcomes. We feel like parents watching their children blossom, and it causes us great joy. In fact, our highest joy is making a positive difference in another person's life. We will take great joy, then, when you find principles of freedom, confidence and personal mastery in the concepts of this book.

Specifically, in this book you will learn:

- Basic principles that govern and explain how you live life
- A model that reveals the nine areas where you get "programmed" resulting in who you are and why you do what you do
- The seven areas necessary for having a balanced life
- How to be completely free from the old "baggage" you have been carrying
- How to change the unwanted aspects of your life – for good

An important point we illuminated in this chapter and one we will revisit and amplify in the next chapter is this: You are a product of your past unless you consciously choose to change. We have said that no two people see the same rainbow. Each person has a unique experience in life and that experience creates a unique perspective about the various aspects of life. And *that* results in how and why you do what you do and are what you are. Because of this, you can cut yourself a little slack and anticipate some hope too.

You never want to blame others—even others in your past for your resulting problems or deficiencies. Blame creates only temporary relief. In addition, often associated with blame is anger, regret, sadness or bitterness. Instead of blame we want to take the posture of understanding.

Since you didn't *decide* to carry the baggage or have the dysfunctional aspects of your nature, you don't need to beat up on yourself or others. Instead, you can go on a quest to find the reasons for your attitudes and behavior. Then, when you do understand, you can use tools to fix or change what is not working well in your life.

Here is something else about this book we think you will appreciate. This is not going to be a book that promises to teach you what is wrong, gives you an answer about what to do, and then tells you to exercise your true grit and make it happen. No, this book takes a much easier approach as is illustrated by the three people we talked about earlier.

A wonderful aspect about the changes that occurred in Janet, John and Betty was that change happened instantly and has been effortlessly maintained. And, no, it wasn't a miracle, though it seemed like it to them and to their friends and family.

The reason for the ease and permanence of change is because it comes from a perception shift, not from focusing on behavioral modification. If perception changes, behavior simply and automatically follows. When you focus just on changing behavior, you need to expend greater strength and more time to create the new habit. Here is an example.

I, Joann, love children. Some would call me a child advocate. I get pretty passionate when I see children mistreated.

One time Bill and I were in Hawaii. It was very early in the morning as we sat on the balcony of our hotel sipping our hot drinks watching the early morning beauty. There was a school across the canal in front of our balcony. I didn't think about what time it was when I saw two or three children sitting on the ground outside a few of the classroom doors.

Because of the "rainbow" of my past, I believed the teachers were not dealing with these children properly. I perceived the situation as one where the teacher had a big class, experienced some unruly children and sent them outside of the classroom. Based on this perception, I began to speak to Bill about my anger. "How could these teachers treat these kids this way? Instead of helping the students, they give them the message of rejection. How do you think that is going to affect them throughout their life…!"

I continued for a bit. When Bill could get a word in edgewise he said, "Honey, it's too early. They just can't get in yet."

"Oh," I said, and my attitude and behavior changed instantly. When my perception changed (parents had to drop their children off early, they were waiting to get into class, this wasn't about unruly children or rejection), my attitude and behavior instantly changed, without effort, and was easily maintained.

This is the kind of experience and process you will find in this book. We will lead you through a process of discovery where you will be able to understand yourself completely. That perception will instantly cause you to be able to put into practice the tools we will teach you which will make your change, your growth, immediately evident and easily maintained.

One more word about your courage. Unless you were just curious or wanted to learn about concepts, you undoubtedly picked up this book to face yourself, learn and grow. The most difficult person to view with total honesty is you. Moreover, the greatest enemy that can prevent you from honestly looking at yourself is... you. We commend your willingness to expose the hidden "you" as well as face the enemy "you" in order to find a more fulfilling life. We give you our handshakes and hugs as we begin our journey.

Chapter 2

The Making of Your Rainbow…

…What Makes You Tick?

It was about 4:00am. I, Bill, had to leave early to catch a plane. Before leaving, I needed to pick up something out of my office. My office was a separate building in the back yard, about 100 feet from the house. Out the sliding glass door, I crossed the deck, followed the stone walkway in the lawn, across the additional open space, to the office. It was raining a bit, yet part of the sky was clear. In front of me a bright, full moon lit up the sky and I could see the clouds that brought the rain.

After getting the file and report I was after, I left the office and headed back to the house. I don't know what made me look over my shoulder but when I did I stopped instantly. I didn't know what to make of it at first. There was…a rainbow?…in the sky. But how could it be? It was dark. Yet the unmistakable shape was there. I stared at it. It looked ghostly, eerie, strange. The colors were the same as you would see in the daytime but they were weaker, sort of washed out.

As I pondered this phenomenon I began to understand what was happening. It was a rainbow, not made from sunlight shining through the raindrops, but from moonlight. Instead of bright sunlight making a bright rainbow, the weaker light of the moon was shining through the raindrops creating this peculiar scene.

The experience moved me. Seeing a large ghostly rainbow set in a dark sky in the middle of the night with a full moon shining behind it created a scene I would not forget. I called it a "moonbow" when I began telling my friends about it. Turns out, though rare, some of them had seen the same kind of thing before.

In the last chapter, we talked about the three dimensions going on at the same time when you see a rainbow. There are the natural laws of physics that are foundational to the making of a rainbow; there is the common experience of people sharing the fact that they are seeing a rainbow (and believe they are all seeing the same rainbow), and there is the third dimension, where *each* person really is seeing a different rainbow, their own personal rainbow.

The very laws of physics that create the rainbow prevent two people from seeing the same rainbow. Light travels at a speed of 186,000 miles per second. Light separates into a predictable spectrum of colors when passing through a prism-like object. The colors are made from different wavelengths of energy. These various wavelengths of light travel in a straight line. Two light-gathering receptacles receiving the light (i.e. two people's eyes) separated by even a small amount of distance pick up different lines of light – thus they receive the light from different rainbows.

An interesting aspect in the application of these laws is this: Even though the basic laws that create a rainbow are unchangeable and constant, the resulting experience from the rainbow that *you* see determines *your* perception and response. Then, generally speaking, different times of day (or night), different locations, and different amounts of rain all can create different experiences in the seeing of a rainbow. The same laws applied during the daytime can create a brilliant spectrum of light. However, when applied at night to create the "moon-bow" they generate a different experience all together.

This is how it works in living our lives. The laws, or principles, that develop our perceptions and reactions about life, our personal rainbow, are few, simple and constant. Yet, these principles are played out differently, in different settings, various relationships, and multiple experiences. Thus, our individual perceptions and reactions to life are as different as each of us is different. As we mentioned before, two people growing up in the same family or with the seemingly same experience as someone else (standing in the same field, supposedly seeing the same rainbow) can have two very different experiences, responses and perspectives.

Donald grew up governed by the basic principles of human behavior we will talk about in this chapter. As a young boy he did not receive, yet hungered for, his father's love and attention. Through a series of circumstances and experiences, he "learned" that dad valued hard work and accomplishment. No one overtly taught him this. Life's experiences gave Donald a clear message, however. "If you are ever going to get dad's attention, you will need to do what he does: work hard, accomplish great things, make a lot of money and be somebody."

When we met Donald, he seemed happy. He was a successful physician, a leader in his church; he, his wife and children were all well liked. Donald was indeed making a lot of money, accomplishing great things inside and outside the health-care profession. He was somebody...to everyone else. To himself, he was still nothing. No matter how hard he tried, no matter what he did, no matter how old he got, he still could not receive his father's love and attention. Outside he was a ball of energy doing wonderful things. Inside he was lonely, sad, a bit angry and did not have a very high opinion of himself. Further, he was stuck in life. He could not even entertain the idea of doing anything differently. He could not live anywhere else, could not consider a different profession or activity within his profession, could not slow down, could not... you get the picture? He was driven inside by this need to be a certain way and do certain things to try and obtain that illusive, necessary parental love. Donald was trapped.

The same principles we are talking about governed Tory too. And she had the same kind of experience as Donald. She too hungered for her father's love and attention. A variety of experiences, some very sad, taught her that her father did not value her. From her perspective, it seemed that her father didn't even want her.

Both Tory and Donald had similar experiences, the wanting of a father's acceptance. Because of the principles of human behavior played out differently for each of them, they had two very different responses. Unlike Donald, a ball of energy constantly trying to accomplish the impossible, Tory was withdrawn, weak, almost lifeless. When we met her, she curled up in the corner of the couch. Her voice was weak and soft. Her posture, energy and behavior like one who had given up on life. Extremely discouraged and hopeless, she was looking for a way out, a way of escape. Unlike Donald who was looking for the top of the mountain, Tory was looking for the mountain to bury her.

How could two people with extremely similar wants and needs, similar experiences turn out so differently? It is because of the similar dynamics and principles in our rainbow analogy. The same principles of human behavior governed them both, but each saw *their own* rainbow in the playing out of these principles creating their individual beings.

The good news is this: Donald and Tory found freedom, happiness and peace when they understood what made them tick, why they had become the way they were, what caused Donald's drive and Tory's collapse. When we taught them how these principles played out in their life and how to live life freely, on purpose, taking control of their own life and future, not living in the past...they both found fulfillment. Donald found peace, and Tory found energy.

To best understand our "self," then, it is important to understand the basic laws or principles that create who we are, then understand the individual, personal ways those principles have played out in our lives. To continue our metaphor, we will understand the laws of physics that create rainbows first (which we will do in this chapter) then we will look at how a specific rainbow (your rainbow) is created within your life experiences.

The Basic Principles that Govern Human Behavior

1. We are products of our past unless we consciously choose to change.

When we are born, we are not given a menu of choices for what we are going to experience. A baby simply receives and engages in whatever comes. With limited repertoire, the baby simply tries to get basic needs such as survival, love, a sense of belonging met as best as possible. How the first experiences go teaches the baby what works and what doesn't work. The baby learns through those experiences. A baby who is spoiled, for example, will tend to continue living out that dynamic throughout life constantly expecting people to come to their attention.

In addition to getting basic needs met, children learn an abundance of facts, conditioned responses, how to relate to certain kinds of people, fears, morals, beliefs, behaviors, ethics, values... and on, and on. And no child ever says, "You know, I'm not sure I like what I'm learning here at home. I think I'll go live down the street with Mr. & Mrs. Smith to see what they teach." Ridiculous, right? Yet the point is a valid one. A child has no option, no choice regarding the enormous amount of learning he or she experiences at a very young age. A child is simply a recipient of what is: without filters, without judgment, without opinion, without the ability to choose anything else.

What a child learns—what you have learned—at a very deep level is not only a "given;" it is *right*; it is *truth*. A rather bizarre, sad example of this is a child who has been raised with physical or emotional pain. The receiving of pain, and the doling out of pain, is "normal" to that child. It is *the* way to relate to others. It is *the* way to give and receive love. This dynamic is like Donald who learned that hard work was the way to get love. He had no other choice before this was illuminated to him. Tory, beaten down and collapsed from constant attempts to receive love, had no choice but to collapse in the presence of others whom she looked up to. She saw no other alternative.

The learning from our past begins at birth (actually it's prenatal in many respects) and continues to accumulate over time, without our choice or control. Naturally, when we are old enough to begin making conscious decisions, we may begin to change some of our beliefs and behavior. That is a part of this first principle, "We are products of our past *unless we consciously choose to change.*" The unfortunate part of this is that most of what we learn is at a deep, subconscious level. When we start making decisions for change, without a full understanding of the principles and dynamics we're going to talk about, those decisions are usually either opposite reactions to our past ("I'm not going to give my children the kind of pain I received." Thus we may give them a better existence but our stance is still reactionary, without the benefit of non-biased perspective), or our choices are dramatically limited by what we have experienced in the past.

We are speaking about this principle in how it affects us negatively. Obviously, this is what we are wanting to look at and change to become free, confident and at peace. The principle is true in *all* aspects of our life, however, even the positive aspects. Let me, Bill, tell you about Joann. (She doesn't necessarily speak of this too often since it may feel like bragging to her...but I'm proud of her, so I will speak of it).

For many of Joann's young and growing up years she was involved in roller-skating. Her days were filled with school, her parents driving many miles to spend hours training with a skating coach. By age 11 she qualified for nationals then continued to bring home first, second or third place trophies at the national level for the next 8 years. The dynamics and perspectives of this athletic pursuit and excellence, a major part of her past, perpetuate into today. Her posture is impeccable. Her persistence with exercise (working out an hour or more, most every day) is so much a part of her she can't even imagine not doing it. How she views her body, her bearing as she walks or dances...all have been positively affected by the experiences of her past.

You are who you are today because of who you were yesterday. Who you were yesterday is because of who you were the day before. How you fix your hair, where you choose to sit when you come into a room, the attitude that is prevalent in you, your perspectives and beliefs about all aspects of life – all came initially from the experiences, events and relationships in your past. That was your school and you have graduated with honors because you have learned perfectly and practice completely the curriculum from your classes.

You are a product of your past *unless you consciously choose to change.* And we will show you how to do that, completely and simply. For now just understand and own this concept. Everything you are and do can be explained by following a trail back in time to find its source.

2. The subconscious mind deals in dynamics, not content.

When I, Bill, was growing up I attended Coffee Creek School, a small, one-room school house in Ferndale, California for the first two years of my school life. One teacher taught all eight grades. Seven students, including myself, attended this school. I was the best student in the second grade! (I am sure you can hear Joann speaking up about now to remind me that I was the *only* student in the second grade).

In this school there were two older sisters who had red hair. These sisters were mean to me. They picked on me and hurt me physically. I was afraid of them. Because I am a product of my past unless I consciously choose to change, I learned that red head girls hurt! I didn't have a choice about this learning. It was an experience I had as a very young child that became implanted in my subconscious.

Many years later, when I was approximately 35 years old, I was in San Francisco entering the office of a female executive on the 20th floor of a high-rise building. As the woman, a red headed woman, walked out of her office to greet me, I was conscious of a bit of resistance inside of me, a vague feeling of fear and a stronger feeling of dislike. I did not succumb to these feelings and continued our conversation, which resulted in my doing some work for her and her firm.

What was going on? The "content" of the moment was that I was dressed in a suit talking to a professional executive in a pleasant, almost elegant surrounding, about training and consulting services I would be delivering. The *"dynamic"* of the moment, however, was me as a little boy in the presence of a red headed woman whom I looked up to. When something looks, sounds, feels, like something from our past, our subconscious views it as though *it is* the same experience as our past and reacts accordingly.

I, Joann, had a coach that would cajole me, almost criticize me, and challenge me by putting me down—all with the motive of trying to push me to do better. I don't work well that way. I didn't like it then. I felt put down, almost demoralized. It made me skate with anger and determination. I skated well but without peace and freedom so I really couldn't do my ultimate best.

To this day, when someone challenges me, puts me down, criticizes me, my initial reaction is to respond exactly like I did with that coach. I've now learned how to deal with this kind of conditioned response, but until I did, whenever I was in this situation I really wasn't dealing objectively with the "content" of the present tense person and situation; I was dealing with my coach.

We have often asked people to do this little visualization exercise. Most people can relate to it. We ask them to imagine having been speeding and a patrolman stops them to give them a ticket. "When the patrolman's light comes on, what do you feel and where do you feel it?" we ask. People report feeling fearful, or maybe angry, and they will feel it somewhere in their body...their head, stomach, neck, head, etc. Then we tell them, "Hold on to the feeling but erase the content of the present scene in your mind. Now let the feeling float backward in time to see what other situations that feeling lands on." Almost invariably and rather immediately, the people see themselves getting in trouble with one of the parents.

What is happening? The "content" of the moment is the person legitimately getting a ticket for speeding. It is a patrolman, not their parent, who is delivering this ticket. Yet the person is reacting, at a visceral level, the same way they did when getting in trouble with a parent. The *dynamics* are the same as the past—an authority figure getting me in trouble—therefore we react, especially at a subconscious level, as we did in the past, because of our perception.

How a person perceives his or her situation greatly determines the internal and external experience and response. Whatever the situation, whatever you believe about it, is true for you. Perception is reality to the perceiver. In a general sense, when you perceive something as positive, you will relate and react to it as positive. The same is true if you perceive something as negative. And this is true about all aspects of the moment. Your internal and external response will be primarily dictated by your perception of reality, which is based on your past experiences, and more specifically, upon the dynamics embedded in that past experience.

This second principle, *the subconscious mind deals in dynamics, not content*, then, simply means that if an experience, event or relationship looks, sounds or feels like something from our past, we will initially react to it with the same perspectives, emotions and responses as we did in the past. There are two unfortunate aspects of this. First, we are limited in our responses to the dynamics of our past; and second, in a very real way, and at a very deep level, we are *living* in the past, constantly perpetuating it by reinforcing the old ways every time we encounter something new that feels like something old.

There is some good news to this principle, however. In following chapters, you will find out how we learn how to react to issues, events, relationships, and experiences in only a few basic areas, nine to be exact. We therefore learn a certain "conditioned response dynamic" in each of these areas. Another way of saying it is, we are "programmed" to respond in a certain way when a certain condition or dynamic occurs.

Here is more good news: We believe, and have seen, that *all* of what we experience in life will find a trail back to one or more of the nine basic programming areas we will talk about later. In other words, when you understand how you learned to respond in the past, in nine basic areas of life, you will understand how and why you respond to all areas of life now. How you learned to respond to survival issues, for example, will be how you respond to anything currently that your subconscious mind perceives as a survival issue; the subconscious mind reacting to the dynamic of the moment, not the current content of the moment which may have nothing to do with survival.

Mike is an example of this. He grew up believing that a multitude of people sticking together is the only way to survive. He learned this in his formative years due to the family "messages" to this effect. "If we stay together, even if someone isn't really fitting in, we will be stronger and can withstand anything. Be loyal, don't betray the family. Stick together at all costs." These were the messages Mike learned growing up.

In Mike's adult professional life, he became the leader and manager of a nine-person team. The content of current reality was that Mike, the manager, had a team of individuals who weren't really working as a team. A couple of people on this team actually, and often, sabotaged the team's success. Many of the team members were not being accountable. Frequently someone would not follow through on a task or a project to the detriment of the team.

What did Mike do? His subconscious mind saw the *dynamics* of the moment as dynamics of survival. In order for Mike to survive this position, thus obtain a salary and have enough income to survive at home, thus making him a successful husband and father so he could survive these relationships...he had to live out the dynamics he had learned. He lived out the messages from his family, "stick together at all costs," which really cost Mike a lot. He was constantly picking up the pieces, doing what others should have done, covering for people to upper management, making excuses for people and generally being over-stressed and overworked, compensating for a rather ineffective, inefficient team.

When he learned that his behavior and interactions were coming from a dynamic of the past, he dealt with it using the tools we will show you later and was able to be a much better leader and manager. His stress level reduced. He stopped overworking to compensate for other's deficiencies. He held people accountable and, over time, the team became a more functional team even weeding out people who didn't work well (Mike was now able to let people go).

Notice how these principles build on each other. The first principle, *we are products of our past unless we consciously choose to change,* states how our past perpetuates into our present and future. The second principle, *the subconscious mind deals in dynamics not content,* tells specifically how our past affects our present and our future. The next principle naturally follows from these two.

3. Everything has meaning and we project that meaning on to others.

As we told you earlier, I, Joann, grew up as an athlete. I trained constantly. The importance of taking care of a person's body was deeply ingrained in me. For me it was a principle of life. I was not born with this belief, however. It came as a result of principle one: *We are products of our past...*

Principle number two: *The subconscious mind deals in dynamics, not content,* also came into play here. Whenever I encountered any dynamic that had to do with health, fitness or well-being, my subconscious, "default mode" was to think about the importance of health and taking care of our bodies. It followed that I would look negatively at myself or others who didn't.

Developing this belief from my past with the accompanying behavior both was a part of the first two principles. It went further, however. At another level, the motivation for following my belief, *why* I did what I did and do what I do was because of the *meaning* associated with this belief and behavior. For me, to not be healthy had major ramifications; I couldn't train; I couldn't compete; I couldn't win.

Though I've learned how to deal with this and change the following rather negative program, before I knew what was going on inside of me, when I saw someone overweight I didn't respect them. Why? The dynamic was one of health, survival, and well-being. My program from the past would fire and I would assume this person wasn't taking care of himself. I placed *meaning* on the moment because of a dynamic from my past. And that would affect my relationship with this person. Fortunately I have learned to not do this anymore.

This third principle about "meaning" is a subtle one (then again, so are all of the principles we are teaching you), but it is the motivation behind our behavior. Everything has meaning to us. Each experience, event, relationship that we encounter has a dynamic we can follow back to some origination in our past. That beginning has some kind of a positive or negative meaning associated with it that we carry forward into the present. And that meaning drives us, toward behavior that perpetuates the positive or behavior that avoids the negative.

This book is about looking at who you are and how you are. Unless you were just curious, you probably picked up this book to find some answers as to why you do certain things or why you feel certain ways. The above three principles may begin giving you a hint of the answers.

Take a look at that fear that hounds you. Take a look at this example of a deep-seated fear and how its true meaning can be teased out by careful questioning of the sequence of responses. "Every time I'm called into the office, even if it is for something positive, I am afraid." What meaning does it have? "What I'm really afraid of is losing my job, not being able to support my family, being a failure..." What dynamic is there? "When I am called to stand before an authority figure, I don't know what they are going to say or want." What past experience is that tied to? "My mother would often tell me that my father wanted to talk to me when he got home from work. She wouldn't tell me what he wanted, and he always had something to yell at me about. And he would often restrict something; watching television, playing with my friends, and many other things."

Hmmm.... The fear of loss associated with being called to the office is the *meaning* built into the *dynamic* of standing before an authority figure which has its roots in the *past experience* of dad calling you on the carpet and your losing something in the experience.

Robert had this kind of experience. When he was very young he lived on a farm and had a dog. He loved that dog. His father was rather mean and would settle conflicts violently. One evening at the dinner table, dad was getting upset because Robert's dog kept barking outside. When Robert saw his father's anger growing into rage, he left the dinner table to take care of the dog. As he was leaving, he heard his father explode in angry words and threaten to get his gun.

Robert ran quickly to find his dog. As he ran around the barn he saw his dog in a corral between the barn and another shed. He continued running toward his dog while his father bellowed out his rage at the dog and at Robert. Robert's fear mounted. His heart was in his throat. He could feel himself shaking as he ran.

Just as he entered the space between the barn and the shed a shot rang out. He dove to the ground. Another shot, then another. The shots barely missed his head. He could hear them, almost feel them, flying by. And with the third shot his dog was dead.

Robert lay there paralyzed in fear not wanting to believe the moment. His young mind raced. He couldn't believe his dad would kill his dog. He couldn't believe his father would shoot the dog when he was so close to it. "Could it be he wanted to shoot me too?"

That experience in Robert's past caused him to have terrible meanings that surrounded the dynamic of conflict. Until he became free of this, he would always do one of two things if he were in conflict. He would either avoid the person completely, or destroy the person. Each response was deeply embedded with anger and fear. Neither response was helpful or even what he wanted. He simply did what he did because of the meaning associated with a dynamic that was similar to an experience in his past.

Everything in your life has this kind of trail, too. How you perceive a certain situation, what you do in that situation, and how you feel about that situation are all results of your past. Again, notice how you are not living in your present when this happens. Instead you are living out your past. Notice also how your behavior or choices of what you will do in a certain situation are limited. You tend to have a reactive response rather than a proactive one.

And that reaction is rooted in the past.

There is another aspect to this principle that effects how you relate to others. Whatever meaning we attribute to something, we tend to believe that perspective is *the* perspective. And others *should* have it too. If, because of our past, we have learned the meaning that people with money are snobbish, we will have a hard time relating to a rich person. If buying new cars instead of used cars is a bad thing, then you will project that meaning onto others and believe that others shouldn't buy new cars either.

We don't mean to imply that this is always the case, but the general principle is true. Whatever beliefs you have based on the meanings you attribute to life will tend to make you think others should have the same perspective. When others don't, that causes relationship difficulties.

Our choices about perspective and behavior, then, are not only limited to how we perceive and respond; they also limit our acceptance of other's perceptions and responses, which further limits how we interact with them.

There is an interesting twist to this limitation on choices, however. Your reaction is not all bad. In fact, according to the next principle, it is good. It is the best thing you can do.

4. Our mind makes the best choice available to it.

Many years ago we read about a study done with some preschool children. It has been so long ago that the concept sticks in our minds without the details of the study, but it went something like this.

Researchers obtained the appropriate permission to do an experiment with very young children. The researcher would place a puppet on each of their hands. They were the kind of puppets that slipped over the hand like a mitten. The puppets were big enough to sit loosely on the researcher's hands, so loose that the child could pull them off easily.

As the researcher would play with a child, the child would reach out for the puppet and invariably pull it off the hand. When the child pulled the puppet off of the researcher's left hand the child would receive a treat that was in that hand. The right hand held no treat.

It wasn't long before the children learned to pull off the left hand puppet. They were readily "programmed" through conditioned response to immediately reach for the left hand, pull the puppet off and receive a treat. Though it has been too long ago to remember the details, a rather overwhelming percentage began pulling off the left hand puppet consistently.

The researchers left the pre-school and didn't interact with the children. After a few weeks they returned with the same hand puppets and the same dynamics, but with one exception; there was no treat in the left hand.

Predictably, most of the children continued to pull off the left hand puppet. They had learned to do it. They had been programmed to do it. When there was no treat they didn't seem upset, however. They just performed the act. They did it…well…just because.

Did these children have a choice about which hand puppet to tug at? Of course they did. How is it that most of them made a pre-programmed choice, then? It is because they didn't have a free choice. They were products of their past (first principle) faced with the same dynamics as before (second principle) driven by the meaning that pulling off the left hand puppet was a good thing (third principle). In other words, they were making the best choice available to them, albeit limited by the first three governing principles.

This illustrates the fourth principle nicely. Our choice about how we interact and what we do in a given situation is limited by the experiences, dynamics and meanings from our past. We do, however, make the best choice available to us.

The reason for this comes from our survival instinct. If you place your hand on a hot stove, you instantly take it off without thought, without even considering your choices. You immediately and automatically make the best choice available to you. It works the same way when you are faced with any decision. Your basic instinct is to protect your relationships, to preserve your livelihood, to maintain your life.

It's rather simple, really, sort of a self-evident truth. When faced with choices, we will automatically make the choice that benefits us the most. That is, benefits us the most *from our perspective.*

One individual might counter-attack a person who is critical while another individual might just sit there and take it. Though the behavior is different based on individual perspective, according to this principle, both people are making the best choice available to each of them. The first person may not have the choice to be receptive because of the necessity of self-protection learned from the dynamics of past experiences. "Taking it" may be synonymous with destruction from this person's point of view. The second person may not have the choice to counter-attack because of wounds received in past experiences when there was an attempt to speak up.

You see, the principle says we make the best choice *available to us,* not the best choice available. The experiences, dynamics and meanings from our past limit our perception and therefore limit our choices. But, limited as they are, within the smaller scope of choices, we still make the best choice available to us within that scope of choices.

From an outside perspective we may think the person is making a ridiculous choice. But that may be because we see a broader scope of choices, a scope of choices the other person cannot see. When we have dealt with suicidal individuals, though we would not see death as a good choice, that person sees death as "the only way out, the best way to get back at so-and-so, the only way to have people see how important I am, to get people to know how much they loved me when they finally miss me…" Suicide is seen as the light at the end of the tunnel. Sad as it is, death becomes the best choice available to a person without many choices.

So whatever it is you have done or are doing, whatever it is that other person is doing, each of you are making the best choice available to you. People aren't out to hurt another person unless it benefits them. The bizarre behavior another person exhibits is coming as a result of some trail of past experience that has perpetuated a dynamic that promotes a specific meaning. That doesn't make the behavior acceptable. But is does make it explainable.

Every time we have worked with an individual, no matter how awful or disturbing the behavior, short of mental illness or organic dysfunction, that behavior has always been the best choice the individual had available to him or her to cope with life. It was always rooted in some positive benefit: survival, identity, protection, pleasure, etc.

So, as you begin looking at your life from the perspective of the first three principles, don't beat yourself up. You, too, have been making the best choice available to you. And that is good news. The key, however, is to recognize that *you do have choice.* You may not believe that yet, and that's ok. We will deal with that concept at greater length later in this book. For now, know that a habit, a conditioned response, a pre-programmed behavior, is a choice. It is probably at a subconscious level, but a choice nevertheless, a choice that has been serving you positively in some way.

An interesting side note to this principle is this: When you recognize or learn that there are other choices that can give you the same benefit, you automatically gravitate to this new behavioral choice. Some people have had profound change quite instantly when they realize this simple fact. *Behavior "X" is serving me in "Y" ways. I can find the same "Y" benefit by doing "Z" and "Z" is easier, more socially acceptable and actually gives me MORE benefits than the primary one. I think I'll do "Z!"* This must be clearly seen and completely believed, however. When it is, change is immediate, sustainable and done with ease. We'll talk about how to do this later.

As we continue to explain the reasons for our behavior and attitude, strengths and weaknesses, fears and joys; you will see how these principles play out in your life in the next few chapters. For now, give yourself a hug of understanding and acceptance realizing you have simply been a product of your past, reacting to past dynamics that repeat themselves in the present, exhibiting behavior resulting from the meanings that surround that dynamic...all the while making the best choices available to you. Recognizing this is a beginning of being able to make new, better choices. It is the beginning of growth.

These four principles govern our behavior. There are four more principles we will talk about in the next chapter that result from these four. The four principles in this chapter *power* our perspective, behavior and attitude. The next four *explain* how these principles play out in our everyday life. Understanding these principles that shape our individual rainbow as well as the next chapter's principles that determine how our personal rainbow manifests itself, all help you become a healthy individual.

Speaking of being healthy, let us introduce you to our concept of health:

> *Health is not the absence of problems; it is the awareness and acceptance of them along with the willingness and ability to deal with them.*

You will never come to a place where you discover that you

have arrived at some state of ultimate perfection. Life is immersed with continued learning and growth. One level of health and well-being is replaced by a higher level. Neither level is the destination, though both are perfect for their time and place.

Your baby is perfectly healthy crawling on the carpet at 10 months old. Your child would not be healthy if that is all she could do when she was 12 years old. It is the same with personal growth. If you are aware of your "self" and possess the willingness and ability to deal with your strengths and weaknesses, you are healthy. If you know what your programs are and are able to deal with them, manage them, and be in control of them instead of them in control of you, you are healthy.

If you are in denial or are not aware of why you do what you do, if you don't know the reason for your attitudes and behavior, if you are controlled by these principles of behavior talked about in this chapter (i.e. controlled by the experiences, dynamics and meanings from your past), you are not healthy. Further, you are not in control of your own life and you are living in the past, living out your past.

We will show you in this book how to have freedom from these powerful dynamics of your past, how to have control of your own life, how to have personal power and confidence as you make your own choices; how to live life freely, on purpose, with purpose...and in this freedom you will find peace. And in this peace you will experience health and well-being.

The road map continues, the explanations become clearer, the answers become real and applicable for *you*, freedom, peace, power and health become yours...turn the page.

Chapter 3

How Does Your Rainbow Shine? ...What Makes You Tick? (Part 2)

Sarah and Jackie were late all the time. I, Bill, hated it. First of all, I am never late. Further, I think it is disrespectful and inefficient when you are late. Every time we were to begin a meeting, start a practice or go to a program, I was always waiting for Sarah and Jackie.

This happened many years ago when I had a singing group and was holding seminars in churches. I was employed to conduct relationship and spiritual seminars in churches. Music was a part of our program. Sarah and Jackie were a part of my music group. And, though they were excellent musicians, they were always late! I hated that!

I did talk to them about it but our discussions never seemed to help. Their tardiness continued and my anger escalated. It wasn't until many years later when I understood the principles in this book that I figured out why Sarah and Jackie's perpetual lateness continued.

We'll tell you what was going on with Sarah and Jackie in Bill's experience above as we explain the four principles in this chapter. These principles are a follow-up to the ones in the previous chapter. The previous four tend to direct our behavior and attitude. The following four principles explain how the previous four play out in our life. They reveal some of the reasons why we do what we do.

Principles that help explain our attitude and behavior:

1. *Anything negative that we hold on to consistently is serving us in a positive way.*

By "negative" we mean something that is troubling, problematic or harmful to you or another person. In the illustration above, Sarah and Jackie's behavior was negative because they were causing problems for other people. Practice couldn't occur until they arrived. Everyone ended up being late to a program because they had to wait for Sarah and Jackie to get to the van so they could drive to the program. Time was wasted, people were inconvenienced and opportunities for relaxed setup were lost due to their lateness. Definitely "negative behavior."

So how could this behavior, that they obviously held on to even after repeated conversations about it, be serving them in a positive way? To understand we need to review the previous chapter's principles. But first, we'll tell you the end of the story so you can see how the principles fit in better.

You see, Sarah and Jackie were hungry for attention. They wanted to "be somebody." Their happiness and identity depended on this. Further, because their fathers (they were not sisters but had the same dynamics and issues in life), the authority figures they wanted attention from, never acknowledged them, they found they could get his attention by rebelling. Nothing extremely bad, just living on the edge a bit, enough to irritate, to cause minor problems...like being late. This behavior became their only choice for having at least some kind of identity, some kind of attention.

Now Sarah and Jackie were in a group of singers (notice, the same dynamics as their interactions with siblings) relating to an authority figure (Bill, the director, the same dynamics as with their father). Do you begin to get the picture? Remember the principles of the previous chapter?

We are products of our past unless we consciously choose to change. Both Sarah and Jackie were living out the way they lived life as young girls. And they certainly weren't consciously choosing to change.

The subconscious mind deals in dynamics, not content. The ***content*** of the current situation was their being in a singing group with time commitments necessary for success and a director who became increasingly irritated with their tardiness. The ***dynamic*** was their being with siblings trying to get attention from their father.

Everything has meaning and we project that meaning on to others. This job and specific appointment to the singing group was important to Sarah and Jackie. In fact, their positions were coveted ones. There were many young people who wanted to be in this group. Sarah, Jackie and the others in the group were chosen after scores of auditions at many colleges and universities.

The subconscious "meaning" they projected on to this situation was this: "This is a special situation. Our director could choose others instead of us. We want to stay on this team so we better make ourselves important. We better do what we can to be somebody, to be special."

Now, here comes the irony. The director, Bill, already thought of them as special musicians. All he wanted was timeliness. To Sarah and Jackie, "special" meant getting attention from Bill. Getting attention meant rebelling—being late was the way they did that. After all, if it was so important to Bill then it became the very focal point for rebellion. The very behavior that could cause them to be terminated was what they used to be special.

Sound ridiculous? At first it does, until you put the first three principles of the last chapter together with the fourth one, and follow it up with the first one in this chapter. (Did you follow that?) Sarah and Jackie were products of their past, acting out the same dynamics in their past because of the meaning they were placing on the present – which also came from their past. Then, the fourth principle of the last chapter...*Our mind makes the best choice available to it.*

Sarah and Jackie were making the only choice available to them to become special, to be important, and to get attention, even though it was negative. They were trapped. So they held on to the negative behavior because it served them in a positive way. The negative behavior was serving them positively by giving them attention, the same kind of attention they got from their fathers.

Do you see how the first principle in this chapter explains their behavior? Their negative behavior was serving them in a positive way. And as we're sure you know, their behavior is all coming from the subconscious mind. When you read about it as we have written it here, it appears to be ridiculous. It is hard to imagine a person acting this way out of clear awareness and choice. If the thought process were conscious, it would be in essence, "Wow, we had better do exactly what Bill doesn't like in order to seem important to him."

As you live life, you probably notice people around you like Sarah and Jackie. You shake your head in disgust or wonder about how they could even imagine doing such a thing. How is it that they could act like that...believe that...want that...? From the outside, other people's attitudes and behaviors seem ridiculous, illogical, and sometimes stupid. But from the inside perspective, the behavior and attitude make perfect sense given the logical trail of cause and effect.

Sarah and Jackie's experience is example of how our inner "programs" can be so illogical, ridiculous or just plain sick. Nevertheless, we all fall prey to them. They creep up on us and cover us. The seed of a behavior-program is planted at a very young age in the soil of experience. It is fertilized by our needs and watered by repeated dynamics. Then it grows, like ivy covering the once bare and beautiful building. We don't choose to be smothered by the jungle of our programs...but we can choose to be free of them. This book is about obtaining this freedom.

As you look at your life you will undoubtedly find behaviors, attitudes or perspectives that appear to be negative to you or someone else. Yet you can't stop them. This principle explains why. At the core of this repeated negativity there is a need being served in a positive way. Granted, it is not the best or most fulfilling way to serve your inner need but it is the best choice available to you. And, relatively speaking, it is positive.

You may be asking, "How could Sarah and Jackie have the exact same experience, attitude and behavior? Isn't that a little far fetched?"

Though their names have been changed, the story is true. We chose this particular story to illustrate the first principle in this chapter so we could introduce you to an interesting phenomenon regarding human behavior. It is this: When you get down to your basic, subconscious programs, there are very few of them, and they are intriguingly similar to other people's programs.

This similarity of programming being true, it remains that there are an infinite variety of ways these programs can be played out. One million people can possess the exact same model of computer with the exact same programs within it. There can be a million ways those computers and their accompanying programs can be used: from developing graphic designs, to running a financial accounting analysis, to writing this book – the same programs utilized and manifested differently. Just like you and your friend and your neighbor. Each of you possesses the same areas of programming yet manifests them in different behaviors and attitudes.

In the next chapter we will show you how this is true, but for now, note that this concept is a bit of good news. If you understand the basic principles, processes, "programs" for growing a garden, though manifested differently, you could grow a garden in many types of locations and climates. Further, if you understand the basics, it is easier to find problems and fix them no matter what location or climate you are in. In essence this truth about similarity in programming makes personal analysis and growth easier.

We have helped many people over the years, each thinking their problem was unique or special. And we have helped them with the same processes, teachings and truths. The problem with thinking your problem is unique or special is that you will tend to be discouraged and helpless, somehow believing that the very uniqueness of your problem eliminates the likelihood of finding a solution. We're here to tell you, that although you are special, your problem or need probably isn't. And, yes, you too, will find the help, the growth you are looking for.

Let's look at the second principle in this chapter that continues to help explain what makes us tick.

2. *Every response is about us.*

Mary did not like where she lived. She nearly hated it. And everyone around her, including her family and friends, knew it. They knew it to the point of misery. They got tired of the complaints, but they felt sorry for her too. Her husband had a great job. Her life was extremely fulfilled. She really lacked nothing. But her complete dislike for where she lived overshadowed everything and made for a very discouraging experience.

What was this really about? Mary would talk about the weather, how cold it was or how dry it was. She would talk about the lack of convenience. Though her community was rather rural and beautiful, she had to drive so far to shop at any quality stores. She would talk about her relationships. Though she had her immediate family living with her (happily we might add) and had some of her closest friends living nearby, and had an abundant amount of acquaintances, she would complain about not being close to the ones she really loved.

And on it went. Nothing was right. Nothing was good enough. The church wasn't what it could be or what she was used to. Her children's school was better where she used to live. Even her car wasn't right for this location. It was too small, not safe enough.

Everything Mary complained about had a lot of legitimacy to it. Either her observations were accurate about another place being better for certain things, or her complaints had legitimacy simply because of preference. But what made her so incessant in her complaints and observations?

There is an interesting principle of life that is a little aside of what we are explaining about this second principle, but you might be interested in it now. Any reaction or response that affects us in a very intense and anxious way is usually an indication that *an internal program is firing.* This is especially true if the reaction is incongruent with the moment. An incongruent reaction, for example, might be if you have greater fear or anger than the situation logically merits. There was no need to throw your entire bag of golf clubs into the lake because you missed the putt. There was no need to avoid all of your friends because you were afraid that one of them might criticize your job decision.

People who have their programs under control, who have found the level of health where they are in control of their programs rather than the programs being in control of them, typically have a more peaceful existence. If there is an intense response in healthy people it usually results from feeling unsafe or unprotected, the desire for love and acceptance, or it is that they are being deeply moved in a positive way.

If Mary knew this, she may have had a clue that her intensely negative response about where she lived was probably ***not*** about where she lived. And, indeed, that was the case. When she came to a Personal Growth Intensive, she learned that her life was filled with trying to get the love and acceptance she didn't get from her mother. The only way she knew to get this love up till her growth in the PGI was to live close to her mother, take care of her mother and thereby receive accolades and monetary gifts from her mother. Further, this was the first time in Mary's life that she moved away from the place where she grew up. Her response, therefore, about her present location was not really about where she lived, (an external focal point), it was about her inner needs and programs.

This is an illustration about what happens in us and to all of us. If you were able to line up 100 people and expose each of them to a legitimate threat, they would all have different responses. Of course, there would be some groupings of people, i.e. those who would fight back, those who would run, those who would logically analyze the threat, those who would be paralyzed with fear, and so on. But even within those groupings there would be nuances of difference in words used, attitude and emotion experienced, and behavioral reaction. Where do these differences come from?

Obviously, given the principles thus far, these reactions are from the individual's past experience which provides the meaning for the moment and dictates the choices available to that person. But the threat remains constant for each of the 100 people. It follows, then, that the response isn't really about the threat, it is about the individual and their past as they relate to the threat.

This gives some interesting ramifications about analyzing ourselves and others as well as benefits in relating to others. First, when intense reactions manifest themselves, instead of looking at the content of the moment, we can follow the trail of the reaction, backward in time, to find the origin of a program that may need some changing. The same can be true in helping us relate to and talk with another individual about their reaction.

A second benefit of understanding this principle is that it can help us not react as strongly to another person's reaction because we now understand that the reaction was not completely about the content of the moment.

Often, there can be a situation where person "A" reacts to person "B." Now, we know that person "B's" response is really about them and not so much about person "A." However, person "A" has an internal response to person "B's" response and reacts to that from some internal program that fires. Then both individuals are *reacting to reactions that are about each of their internal programs,* and the focus on the real and beginning issue is gone.

Clyde and Olga fell victim to this trap. They worked in a hospital. Clyde, a physician, violently reacted to a patient not receiving the care he thought should be administered. Olga reacted just as violently because of her belief about what should be done with this patient.

It turns out Clyde was re-living a survival program from his Vietnam days where he felt trapped, violated, fearful and incensed over trying to treat young boys who were maimed or dying in a situation he believed shouldn't even exist in the first place.

Olga was re-living an identity program from her young nursing days of never being listened to, not being given respect—and actually experiencing this in the context of relating to an incompetent doctor.

Clyde's response was about Clyde. Olga's response was about Olga. Neither of their responses was about patient care. *Every response is about us.*

Understanding this can reap a more empathetic and understanding response toward others. It can help us stay focused on real issues rather than getting sucked into reacting about reactions. It can make us more neutral or objective when we receive the brunt of someone else's reaction, keeping us from placing a meaning from our own past on to the current response of the other person.

Understanding this principle can provide a trail to walk backwards in time to where a program that initiated the response originated. And doing that can give you a place to use the tools you will learn in this book to find freedom from these knee-jerk responses that come from inappropriate or no longer needed programs.

3. *Feelings are indicators or responses; they do not dictate reality or truth.*

I, Joann, want to speak a bit about this principle. I understand it well and have learned a great deal about how to benefit from it.

I am very much in touch with the kinesthetic aspect of life. Because of my athletic background in my young days, my emphasis in personal training for many years thereafter, my natural intuitiveness and the way I am emotionally and physically made, I am extremely aware of body and emotion.

Within seconds of meeting someone or just watching them walk by, I can tell what muscular or skeletal problems the person may be having. I can get a good idea of how the person is feeling. And I certainly can tell you what they are wearing, from their hair color and style down to their type of shoes. Bill, on the other hand, though he is extremely good at reading people, has to do it a bit more consciously. Sometimes he doesn't even notice if one of our friends got a hair cut. (I always tell him when I'm getting mine cut).

This is not a problem. Nor is it a statement of right/wrong, good/bad or effective/ineffective. It is just describing a difference.

Now, some people, like me, who are really in touch with their feelings, live on that level. Their feelings determine reality and truth. Some people make decisions, judge value or experience happiness based on how they feel. This can be a real problem.

Feelings can come from three main sources: 1) Physiological states of being, 2) reactions to present situations that result from past-generated, internal programs, and 3) reactions to present situations.

Physiology can play a major role in generating feelings. Depression can be a pre-cursor to illness. Fatigue can make you irritable. So can not breathing deeply enough to obtain enough oxygen or not drinking enough water. Lack of exercise can make you feel lethargic. And, my personal favorite, hormones (mostly in women but men can experience them too) can give you a roller coaster ride of emotional instability.

I am sure you already have seen how our internal programs can cause reactions, complete with pre-designed behavior and emotion. And, we've noticed that most people, when they look at their day-to-day interactions with life are experiencing feelings that come mostly from internal programs that have not been found or managed. The anger feeling Clyde had was not coming from his current reality. It was coming from a survival program deeply embedded from long ago.

So, feelings can come from physiologically based origins or reactions from internal programs. At best, feelings result from some current reality and are indicators of either danger, pleasure, intimacy or some other natural response arising from a natural occurrence. These kinds of feelings should not be ignored. A feeling of danger or fear is an indicator that is your friend and motivator towards dealing with some legitimate threat. The feeling of love or joy in closeness with another person is an indicator that these feelings need to be followed or expressed so as to develop or strengthen that relationship.

In any case, the feeling is a *result* of something else. *Feelings don't generate reality, reality generates feeling* – even if it is a past reality, a misconception of reality, an internal physiological reality. So to live on the level of feelings, to give feelings the power to empower attitude or action, is to live life at least one step removed from reality. This can create undue stress, worry, or anxiety, and it certainly can have damaging effects on relationships. Yet many people do just that—living as though feelings meant more than simply being an indicator or response.

Here is what we do when we are living on the level of feelings rather than fact: We can tend to judge the quality and content of our surroundings, or our current reality, including our relationships, based on how we *feel* about that reality or relationship. And this is unfair.

If you *feel* depressed because of some pre-sickness state, you don't know that it is a pre-sickness state so you have to make sense out of it somehow. How do you do that? You say, "I am depressed because...." Then you finish the sentence with the most logical or local person or situation that could potentially explain the depression. Your husband didn't kiss you goodbye this morning when leaving for work. Johnny didn't clean his room like you told him too. Your cake fell before the baking was complete. Something, anything, is a potential candidate to receive the "you-are-the-cause-of-my-depression" award.

Further exacerbating the problem is this: the explanation you have come up with may make some sense. You then react to this logical conclusion by giving your husband the cold shoulder, yelling at Johnny or vowing to never bake again. Then people react to your reaction thus amplifying the problem further. And it all stems from your giving validity and meaning to a feeling that was really nothing more than an indicator or response. You have given the feeling too much meaning.

You also know that feelings can change quickly, dramatically and without logic, which can create even more confusion and frustration. When someone is inconsistent or incongruent in reaction or relationship it creates what the psychology field calls "crazy makers." And crazy makers...make us crazy.

So what do you do? Look at the principle again: *Feelings are indicators or responses; they do not dictate reality.* We teach people to recognize that feelings are important. They are even necessary. Life is richer because of feelings. Life would be empty without them. Imagine a love relationship without the feeling of love. Not a very fulfilling experience. But *feelings don't determine the facts; facts determine feelings.*

Another important point to understand is that feelings *must* be expressed. Feelings that are not expressed are stored in our body, in our memory and in our emotional scrap book. The only way to rid ourselves of this emotional baggage is to express those feelings in a safe way to a safe person. If we don't, time does not eradicate the feelings, but they do come out. And they usually come out inappropriately or incongruently.

Stored feelings that attempt to seep out may find themselves manifested physiologically in the form of inexplicable pain or recurring sickness. I, Bill, had a client in my counseling practice who was referred to me by a physician. She had been through every test available to try to find and diagnose a constant pain in her upper back and shoulder. There seemed to be nothing medically wrong with her. After working with this young woman for awhile I found that she had been sexually molested when she was a child. Her feelings of pain, violation, guilt, and fear were never expressed and found their way manifested as physical pain. After therapeutically freeing her from this experience and its effects, the pain went away and never returned.

So, we are to embrace and express our feelings, openly, with tact and sensitivity, but we also must put feelings in their place. They are not necessarily truth. We teach people to look at truth and let truth, accompanied by choice, determine decision and direction. Feelings, then, become the beautiful mantle of feathers the eagle wears as it soars high in the winds of freedom. Powerful gusts of wind may ruffle the eagle's feathers and he feels that. But it is the eagle's clear vision of reality and not the ruffling wind that determines how it spreads the feathers in his wings to fly. The feathers don't dictate the flight, they facilitate it.

4. "Fuzzy Logic" principles govern our perspective and behavior.

Not too many people are familiar with the term "fuzzy logic" but most of us are in contact with its technology daily. It is a term created in July, 1964 by Lotfi Zadeh, a University of California Berkeley Professor. Its description and explanation parallels how our mind works with its neural network of patterns and processes.

You may wonder why we are introducing this technology within a book on personal development and growth. "Does it have application?" you ask. And indeed it does. In fact, Bill's study of fuzzy logic lead to the development of the powerful programming model you will learn about in the next chapter. This model claims to explain and predict all human behavior and attitude—and it does. It has been successfully doing so since 1996. Also, the understanding of this concept will further help you understand what makes you tick.

Let's begin our explanation by building an understanding of how typical, binary computers are programmed. There is a huge series of if/then statements that if diagrammed on paper would look like an incredibly long flow chart of multiple forks in the road. The computer's program asks a series of sequential questions. For purpose of illustration we will make them questions that would have an answer of either yes or no. Then the computer is programmed to follow the logic of this: "If yes, then…. (a pre-designed action)." Or, "If no, then… (a pre-designed action)." And the sequence continues. The next question rises from the previous answer.

Fuzzy logic computers are based on a different type of "logic." It can be explained with the example of coming home from work, walking into the front room and deciding where to set the temperature on the forced-air heater. There are only a few things to consider: What time is it? How do I feel? Am I having company? What is the temperature outside? ...and maybe a few more considerations.

You can readily see there are an infinite number of outcomes to the question about where to place the thermostat depending on the answers to these very few questions. If it is 10:00pm, and you are going to bed in a half hour, and it is 67 degrees outside, you would place the temperature control in a different place than if it is 4:00pm, you are having company come over for dinner, and it is 39 degrees outside.

This is the "logic" behind "fuzzy logic" being called "fuzzy." The binary programming has clear, crisp questions and answers. A very focused question which can only have two possible answers. This necessitates an inordinately long list of questions to come to an ultimate conclusion.

A small list of questions, all considered at the same time, for a composite picture and resulting decision is less crisp and precise, but more efficient and flexible. And there are a multitude of applications we all experience frequently that binary computers couldn't do. One-button microwave ovens, "more dry" – "less dry" controls on clothes dryers, the feature in video cameras that holds the image steady – all are done by a fuzzy logic computer chip operating in the appliance or electronic device.

The core concept is this: for everything there are a few, and usually a *very* few, considerations *made at the same time* that produce an outcome. This is how we function in our daily interaction with life too.

Let's create a simple example. Imagine a mother interacting with her child who is in life-threatening danger, both to the mother and the child. Let's also say that there are only three programs running in the mother, one for personal survival, one for identity and self-esteem, and a spiritual program of selfless love. Our concept in this principle is that all of these programs will fire *at the same time* and create an outcome.

Depending on the mother's level of health and past programming, the outcome of her attitude and behavior will be affected. If her survival program is being driven by deep fear stemming from past near-death experiences, that may paralyze her. Her self-sacrificing love program may cause her to ignore everything else and save the child even in the face of life-threatening risk. If there is an extremely selfish identity and self-esteem program that says she must look good at all costs, that program may drive her to save the child even in the face of fear and lack of selfless love.

While this illustration is obviously too simplistic to replicate real life, we trust that you can see the point. Many of our programs fire together and create an outcome of behavior and attitude. And, though there may be only a few programs that are running in you at the same time, there is virtually an unlimited amount of outcomes you can experience because each of the programs have an unlimited level of health and perspective and there are even more combinations of how these programs interact together. This is what creates so many individuals from so few programming areas.

You are going to learn in the next chapter that there are nine areas you develop programs within. These nine areas fire at the same time to produce an outcome. The good news is this: If you understand your program in each of these nine areas, you can understand why you do what you do in any given situation. Further, you can actually *predict* what you *would* do in a given situation because you would know what programs would fire and how they would affect you.

Are you ready to look at your inner programs? This has been an exciting process for us over the years. Some people approach it with fear. They are a bit anxious about what they will find. Here is what we tell them, and what we tell you. You are already functioning in certain ways in life. Unfortunately for most people, that functioning is a result of unidentified programs that are in control of you. The exploration that will begin in the next chapter will help you find your programs and develop an even deeper understanding of why you are the way you are and why you do the things you do. Following chapters will teach you how to change *anything* you find that you don't want or like. So the exploration is not a hopeless one, it is, in fact, hope-filled.

You won't discover problems without solutions. Instead you find answers to riddles, reasons for responses, and best of all, freedom from fears and bondage and baggage and blame. Exciting discovery begins in the next chapter. Complete freedom comes soon after.

Chapter 4

Your Programs

...Where your habits and attitudes begin

Mike called home. "I'm free," he said.

"How did you get that way?" his wife asked.

"I found out where my problems were, my programs, and changed them." This was Mike's experience after a Personal Growth Intensive.

Sound too simple? Well, it is simple but it is not necessarily easy. Based on everything we've said so far, you can probably see how strong the inertial effect of our past is. When you learn something important or significant, you typically learn it at a very deep level. And it is hard to unlearn it.

Remember learning how to ride a two-wheel bicycle? Someone showed you how to do it, your Mother, Father, Brother...someone who already knew how. This person gave you instructions: "Hold your hands here. Sit this way. Don't turn the handle bars, lean into the corners. Keep peddling." Then he or she supported you while you got on the bike (without training wheels) and pushed you off.

Remember your fear? Remember how bad it felt when you went down and skinned your knee or elbow? Remember how big you grinned when you were able to go a hundred yards without falling? Remember how confident you felt when you mastered the skill? Remember how you felt when you could ride as fast as the wind and go places on your new symbol of freedom?

Now…try to ***unlearn*** how to ride a bicycle. It would seem impossible, right? And, though unlikely, it is possible. More realistically, however, it is very possible to not have the bicycle have a place in your life anymore.

The trick is not to ***unlearn*** how to ride a bike. The trick is to ***learn*** how to have something take its place. The key is finding how you learned it in the first place, maybe even why you learned it in the first place, then ***replacing that learning*** with something different or better.

This re-learning concept is based on the principle: *You cannot remember to forget, but you can forget to remember.*

You cannot forget to think of a watermelon while focusing on trying to forget the watermelon. Every time you say to yourself, "I must not think of a watermelon!" or "I choose not to think of a watermelon!" what have you done? Right. You have just thought of a watermelon. The only way you can forget the watermelon is to replace the thought of a watermelon with something else. Focusing on the mantra or image, "I choose to think of a mountain," then seeing clearly its majestic imagery, the cool breeze, the beautiful colors, the refreshing sounds…will automatically stop you from thinking about a watermelon. The mountain has replaced it.

This is a simple illustration but powerful in its core dynamics. Let's take this concept into our bicycle analogy and press the point of symbolism so as to nail down an important concept.

Imagine sitting in your garage every day, starring at your bike, working hard to forget about your bicycle. It wouldn't work. What would work, however, is this: "I have been riding my bicycle for many years. I enjoy it but the main reason I learned to ride it was to get around town more quickly. I have a driver's license now. I can use a car instead of my bike and thereby go faster and farther. I choose to use my car instead of my bike."

Then, each day, as you go to the garage and choose your car instead of your bike, the car replaces the bike. You may never unlearn how to ride a bike but your desire and ability will diminish over time with your new found ***replacement*** behavior.

A key element here is that the replacement must be something that at the least satisfies your need in the same way, and *more preferably*, in a better way. This will naturally cause you to gravitate to the better choice and behavior. And, though simple in its illustration, again notice this dynamic: After you possessed a car or the use of one, how many times did you have to consciously choose to use your car instead of your bike? How much effort did it take? It was no effort at all, was it?

The dynamics in these simple analogies are what Mike was referring to when he called his wife. For years he had habitually engaged in life in the same way, with the same attitudes, fears and behaviors. He didn't even know why he did it or how he developed these traits. He was habitually riding his bike through life knowing there was a better way but didn't really know what it was or how to obtain it.

Through understanding the basic principles in the previous chapters and the resulting programs found in this chapter, he saw very clearly what he was doing, why he was doing it and what he wanted to change. He then became "free" because he no longer had programs controlling him. Rather, he was in control of them. Symbolically speaking, he was now able to freely choose whether to ride his bike or drive his car. He didn't keep riding the bike out of habit.

The previous chapter's principles give you the basic reasons for why we do what we do, but what about those specific behaviors, habits, fears, attitudes, and responses? Do you notice how people have the same issues they are dealing with all their life? And they are relatively few, right? One person may have constant rebellion toward authority, abrasive interpersonal skills, and fears about her future financial security. Another person may be too submissive to everyone around, allowing others to take advantage of him, though he may be extremely strong willed when it comes to taking care of the underdog, continually giving, even to the point of personal poverty.

As you look at your life, do you notice how you are always doing the same things over and over again? Do you notice you are always dealing with the same issues in life, the same fears, the same needs, the same wants? Do you notice how you keep kicking yourself about the same mistakes and behavioral blunders?

Where do these behaviors, fears and attitudes come from? They come from specific programs that are firing in us. It is like the software in a computer. The parameters of how the computer works (processor speed, types of programs running, size of memory, etc.) symbolize the principles we talked about in the previous chapters. The specific way a program is functioning parallels the specific behaviors and attitudes with which you are functioning.

This chapter will reveal a model that explains the nine basic areas within which we develop programs. It will show you where your basic, habitual behaviors and attitudes come from. But we're not going to leave you there. We will show you how to specifically find your programs and reprogram them to how you want them to be in chapter six. For now we will show you the model and how it can explain and predict your behavior and attitudes.

And here is some good news: Based on your understanding of the foundational psychological principles of behavior in the previous chapters and your knowledge of the basic programming model in this chapter, you will have a rather complete picture of who you are, why you do the things you do, and how it is that you hang on to unwanted behaviors and attitudes.

I, Bill, will now take the lead in explaining the model in this chapter because I want to tell you the history behind it and how it came to be.

I have always tried to figure out why things are the way they are. From the natural sciences to human behavior, at an early age I wanted to understand what made things work and why they worked the way they did. And I did a lot of experimenting, questioning and reading to find answers.

When I was seven or eight years old, I remember going to the kitchen junk drawer (you know, every house has one) and finding a flashlight bulb in there. I then found a battery, a spring from a birdcage and a hammer. My young mind reasoned that with a bulb, a battery (a source of electricity) a spring (a metal wire that I somehow knew was important for conductivity) and a hammer (every scientist needs tools)..., with all of that I should be able to make the light bulb shine. My mother said I would sit for a long time and work on this "puzzle." And I can remember pondering over it at the metal kitchen table, sitting on the chrome framed, padded chair that would look today like it came straight out of a 1950's diner.

I remember experimenting with travel. As soon as I learned that the earth was spinning, I went out into the field and jumped up and down on a large dandelion plant. I reasoned that I should be able to travel as the earth moved under my feet while it spun. I didn't understand the principle of inertia at the time. (I felt good when later in life when I found that Richard Feynman, one of the world's leading physicists, did the same thing when he was young).

By the time I was a teenager, I was cross pollinating plants and working a small meteorological station while reading about the basic psychology of human behavior. This quest for understanding led me to ask many questions throughout my undergraduate and graduate studies. I was never satisfied with the models that existed. They explained many aspects of our selves but didn't seem to be all conclusive or practically helpful in all situations.

I learned about a valuable practice from reading about Einstein. His profound theories came from looking for the answer to simple, almost childlike, questions. "What would things look like if you could travel as fast as a beam of light?" for example. I began to ask simple and basic questions too. "What would cause a person to act the same way every time he or she encountered the same circumstance? Where did that behavior come from? Is there a basic law that governs ***all*** behavior and response? If so, is it applicable to all people?"

The models I studied, from Jung to Maslowe, from Freud to Erickson, and many others didn't fully satisfy me. The concepts I read about encompassed many models including deep, subconscious archetypical programming, the pleasure-pain model, the need to fulfill a basic set of needs, family systems—all seemed to make meaningful contribution to "the answer" but, for me, didn't seem simple enough or practical enough to explain or help in all cases.

And, admittedly, I was looking for Einstein's equivalent of a TOE, the Theory of Everything. He could only boil the universal laws down to a basic few with different ones explaining different actions. There was the electromagnetic force explaining the behavior of magnetism and electricity. There were the strong and weak nuclear forces explaining the nuclear power/matter relationship in his famous formula $E=MC^2$. And there was the force of gravity explaining how objects are attracted to each other. He theorized, however, that there was a deeper, more simplistic explanation or theory, a Theory of Everything, that could bring all four of the above mentioned theories into one and have one set of explanations and predictions. But he never found it.

I, too, searched for a Theory of Everything in regards to a psychological, behavioral model. Each of the models and theories I studied had great history, merit and benefit in explanation and prediction. But could there be something more basic, something that would encompass the others, not replacing their value but transcending it?

I recognized the naivety with which I could be approaching this. Further, I understood the egotistical inference this very question posed. Who was I to question the great masters of psychology? Who was I to want to go beyond the models and theories that already were time tested and valuable? Yet, I humbly set those inferences aside and started my quest. At best, I would find something. At worst I would learn something.

I will explain the model, therefore, in the context of my quest. And I will tell you this; after completing the model and testing it for a time, I took a group of people to a combination work/play seminar in Hawaii. Our agenda was to spend each morning in explanation and testing of this model. They helped fine-tune a few points in it. From that time on, we have been using it with great satisfaction and remarkable results. But, now, back to the quest.

My first conclusion was this: All behavior comes from beliefs. My conclusions came from studying a vast amount of writings plus reflection on personal experience as well as the experience of my clients. (I had a counseling practice at the time). Additionally, the conclusions came from my sifting through theories and hypotheses that I would develop then discard if they had no merit. Finally, my conclusions became what people referred to as "self-evident truths," concepts that made sense even if untested and untried in an individual's experience.

In fact, self-evident truths seem to have power because they explain what a person already knows, either intuitively or experientially. When Columbus concluded that the earth was round it explained what he already knew to be true, for instance, ships' sails seemed to go over the horizon, the sun seemed to go around in a circle during the day, wouldn't it seem logical that it would during the night too, etc. Thus, "the earth is round" became a self-evident truth that was believed with great conviction even before it was tested. Einstein had many of these self-evident truths, "theories," as well. For years his theories were believed even before they were verified or could even be tested. They made sense and explained many mysteries in the universe – though it was only after many years that the equipment was invented or perfected to the point that his theories could be tested.

Thus, my first theory or self-evident truth, my first conclusion was "A person's actions result from beliefs." When you enter a room, when you encounter a given situation, when you are in the presence of a certain type of person, you have certain beliefs that result in behavior. I know now that this concept is more fully explained by the principles in the second and third chapters. We are products of our past. And that creates certain beliefs about a new encounter with a situation that has the same dynamics as the previous one. And that results in our behavior.

A diagram of this very rudimentary model is shown on the next page in figure 4.1.

"Now," I foolishly said, "If I can find ***the*** basic beliefs all people have, I can understand, explain and predict all behavior." And so I began searching for some basic belief system all people had or should have. (I was optimistic but initially naive in my search). Needless to say, I did not find a set of beliefs everyone had. What I did find was where our beliefs come from.

Another way of saying this is, I found nine categories where the basic principles we have already talked about are played out and that create our programs—the cause and effect belief systems that create our behavior. "If I encounter 'X' it has the same dynam-

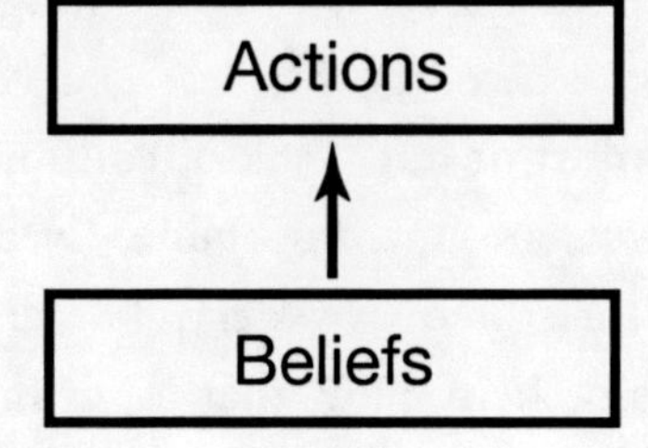

FIGURE 4.1

ics as a previous experience I have had, 'Y,' and thus causes me to react in the same way as before. I thus experience the attitude and behavior of 'X' because I am a product of my past. Or, in other words, 'X' looks like 'Y' so I behave like 'X.'"

And as has been said before, I believe that all experiences in life fit within one of the nine categories in this model. Thus, if you understand your basic programs in these nine areas you can understand yourself fully. Plus, you can predict how you will be and what you will do for future situations.

The first, most basic area of programming concerns our survival. As a young child we begin to learn survival tactics through what causes us comfort or not. Lack of comfort can be translated into threat. When we are uncomfortable, (wet, hungry, in pain), we feel threatened or scared so we cry. The crying is our way of reaching out for some help. How that cry is met begins to tell us what we need to do to survive.

If we are spanked or disciplined in some way that can result in believing that we should not reach out if we have need. The hurt we receive by reaching out is worse than the hurt, pain or discomfort that comes from hunger or wet diapers. This belief is at the core of a behavior that creates a program. Every time we experience a need, whether we are 2 years old, 20 years old or 60 years old, we don't reach out. We have been programmed not to. Have you ever seen someone like this? Someone who never reaches out for another person's help? This may be one of the reasons why.

Another child may get ***too much*** care when he or she cries out. Instead of just changing the diaper, the mother holds the child, feeds the child, plays with the child, gives the child treats—and goes beyond normal care and love; she spoils the child. This kind of programming can result in the child never having the incentive or need to take care of self. Instead the child goes through life expecting others to take care of everything.

Obviously these two examples may be a bit extreme. The point remains, however. What you learn as a little child regarding survival tactics creates beliefs that result in behavior and attitudinal programs. And the learning is cumulative.

As a child experiences the same dynamics over and over, the belief is more completely confirmed and the program is more deeply embedded. The program continues to play out with ever increasing inertia, outside the awareness of the person continuing to grow in power and prevalence.

My mother has an interesting survival program. She was the first child born in America to a Portuguese family. It was a large family. She was born pre-maturely and put in a shoe box at home. Because of her weak beginning, and because she was raised in a large family who was poor, needing an abundance of food has always been a part of her survival program. Two or three families could find enough food in her house to last them a month. When Mom cooks dinner, there is always more than enough. It is not uncommon for her to have two or three entrees, a green salad, a Jello salad, a pasta salad, corn, peas and potatoes, plus two or three dessert choices—and this is just for Joann and me! The abundance of food is probably not a style or preference issue, it is probably coming from a survival program that is firing that has at its core the belief, "If we don't have enough food, we'll die."

And, obviously, this belief is not literal at the moment. It is simply an inertial belief from long ago. It comes from experiencing the same dynamics as the survival dynamics in early childhood. So, until Mom understands this dynamic, she is a product of her past and has no other choice but to have and cook a lot of food if she wants to feel secure and fulfilled in response to this program.

Remember Mike in chapter two? His survival program came with the belief that there must be many people around. He put up with incompetence, lack of accountability and a host of other inappropriate behaviors in his staff. His reason? His stated reason was that he was trying to be a caring leader. After he understood about programs he more clearly understood the real reason. It was because a survival program was firing.

Clyde, in chapter three, living out the survival dynamics of his Vietnam days is another example. He had the inappropriate behavior of yelling at staff and throwing instruments, justifying it with some legitimate logic surrounding patient care, but in reality, the behavior was coming from a survival program learned long ago, still firing today.

So, survival is a very powerful arena within which we learn behavioral beliefs that are perpetuated in programs that result in the actions on our programming model.

I've focused more on the area of survival in this chapter than the other areas in this model. This is to give you an idea of how this model works. The real purpose of this chapter, however, is to teach you what the model is and give you an introductory idea of how it works. In chapter six you will learn how to find all of your specific programs in the various programming areas in this model and how to reprogram the unwanted ones.

You may notice now, however, how the model may explain some of your recurring attitudes or responses with the associated behavior. If you do, that's great. But don't worry about doing anything about it yet. Just note that those recurring behaviors are coming from some prevalent program created in you at an early age. For now, just focus on understanding the model and how it reveals and predicts behavior and attitude.

Figure 4.2 on the next page shows how survival fits into our basic programming model.

The next area of programming comes in the context of our <u>identity and belonging</u>—who are we and where do we fit?

Basic Programming Model

Actions

Beliefs

Survival

FIGURE 4.2

Like survival, this is another powerful area of programming. This is where we learn how to be liked and loved. It is where our self-esteem is embedded. It is where we get our sense of belonging and value and worth. It is where we learn all of our social skills and our ability to interact with others. But really, all of the interactions, skills and behaviors alluded to in the previous paragraph flow out of one basic concept – our view of self, our self-esteem. How we see ourselves, our belief about who we are and how (or if?) we fit, results in our attitude toward self, and how we engage with other people.

In a very interesting way, we have found that this area of programming is even more powerful than survival programs for most people. This is probably because most people's survival needs are generally and adequately met. We have also found that most people ***do not*** have the needs in the identity/belonging area fully met. Most people are walking through life hungry for love and acceptance, not hungry for food and shelter. In fact, give most people a survival scenario and they will wish for someone to be there with them, not so much for help, but for the belonging dynamics that makes it easier to endure.

This area of programming is so powerful and needs such amplified explanation and attention that we're going to dedicate an entire chapter to it. Chapter five, the next chapter, will teach you about your self-esteem, your identity and belonging programs in great depth. We will also show you how to have a healthy self-esteem and confidence in your interactions. Further, you will learn how to have peace and freedom from fear as you engage with others. For now, understand that identity/belonging is the second area of programming. These two areas, survival and identity/belonging, are the two most powerful programming areas in this model. They are so powerful, we call them drivers. The beliefs or programs you have in these two areas are driving most everything you do.

Figure 4.3 on the next page depicts this relationship.

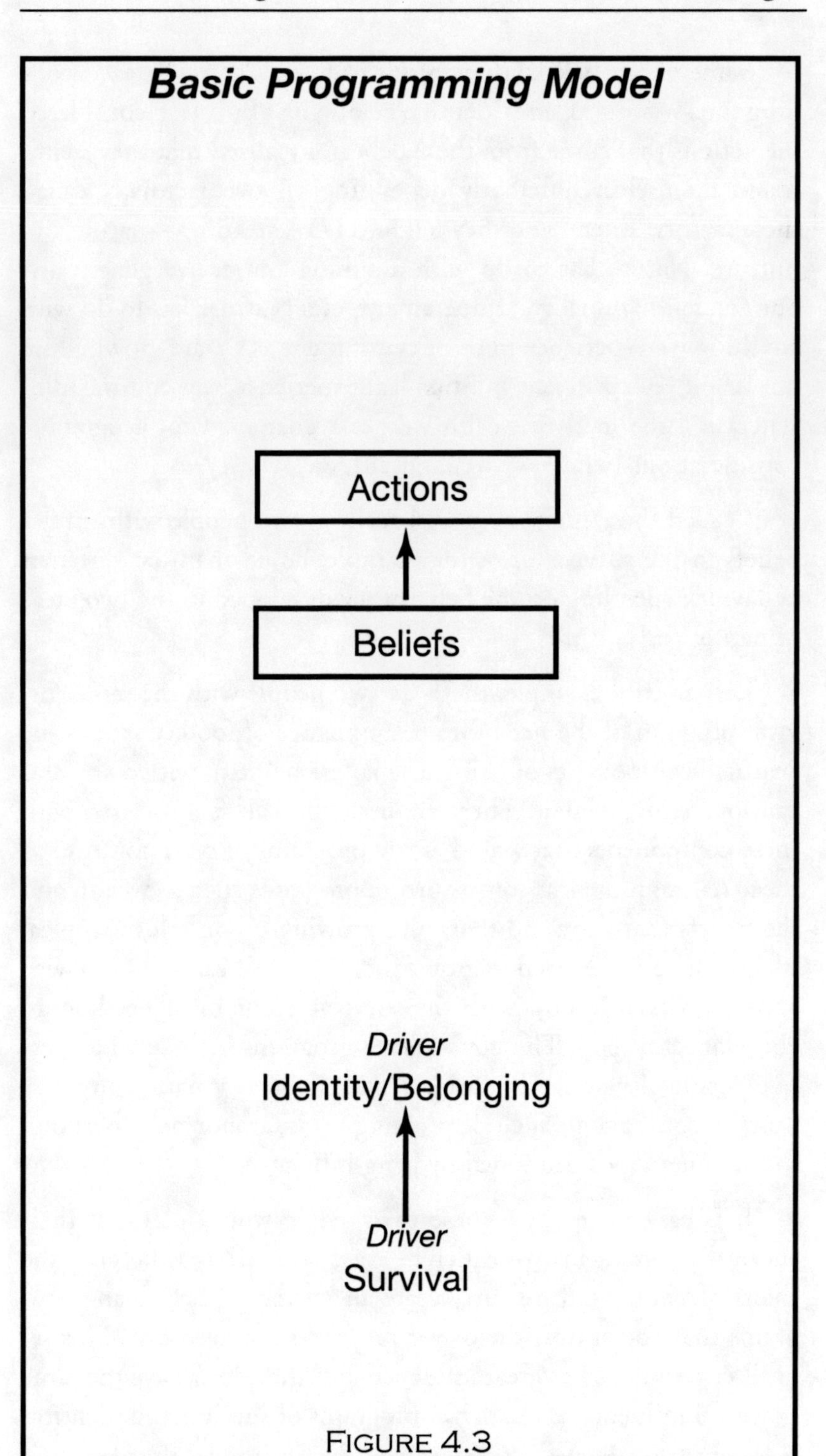
Basic Programming Model
Actions
Beliefs
Driver
Identity/Belonging
Driver
Survival

FIGURE 4.3

Some of our beliefs, then, result from the "driver" areas of our programs—survival and identity/belonging. But as I considered the actions that come from these beliefs, I realized that they manifested themselves differently depending on two factors. I called these factors "filters" and they fell into two categories—nature and nurture. Nature has to do with anything we receive genetically: our gender, nationality, temperament, etc. Nurture has to do with anything we experience in our environment as we are growing up: our first love experience, our first fear experience, our cultural idiosyncrasies, the level of wealth we get accustomed to, geographic considerations (where we were raised), etc.

I called these filters because I realized two people with similar beliefs in the survival area, for example, could manifest different behavior depending on the beliefs they developed in the two areas of nature and nurture.

Let's say, for example, there are two people with the same survival program of the need for an abundance of food. One has the "nature" components of being a Japanese woman, with a shy and cautious temperament. There are certainly beliefs associated with these components that would create programs of behavior. Add to those nature programs some nurture programs such as wealth and the beliefs that surround that, plus growing up on a lush tropical island where she learned to grow food. Contrast that scenario with another person, a boy, with the survival program of needing an abundance of food. The boy's nature programs include an aggressive personality and being a New York Italian by nationality. His nurture components include growing up in a poor neighborhood in the inner city surrounded by gang influence.

It is easy to see how these two people would play out their survival program in two different ways, isn't it? It is because the filters of nature and nurture create an overlay of beliefs and programs that adjust how the driver programs are lived out. This set of filter programs has great influence, but they don't have the same powerful influence as the driver programs of survival and identity/belonging. See Figure 4.4, next page, for our model thus far.

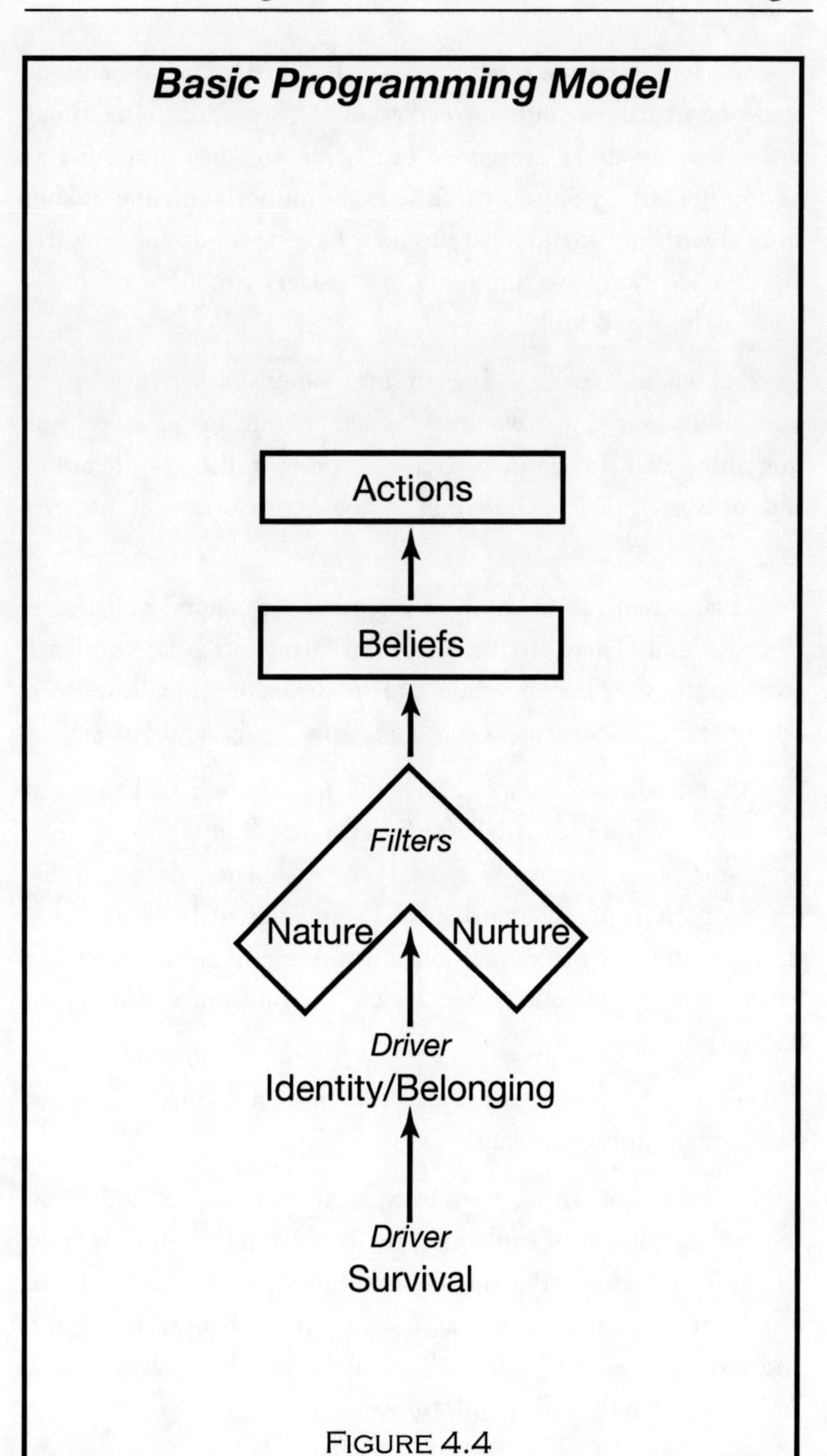
Basic Programming Model
Actions
Beliefs
Filters
Nature
Nurture
Driver
Identity/Belonging
Driver
Survival

FIGURE 4.4

As I looked at the model thus far I realized a lot of behavior could be explained, but not everything. I began thinking about and observing other aspects of our being and behavior such as having fun. I have always had a sense of humor and enjoy joking around with my friends. Joann and I have a wonderful time living life. We even have fun going to a grocery store. For us, life is meaningful—and fun!

"So, where does "fun" fit in to this model?" I asked myself, and realized that it didn't. I wondered whether "fun" or "pleasure" was something that drove our behavior. But after much consideration and conversation I realized that it doesn't drive us – it ***attracts*** us.

This caused me to think about other "attractors" and this is what I found: There are three types of "attractors" that we all are attracted to. One may have more of an attraction but all three can be attractive. These attractors are: Pleasure, Peace, and Power.

After finding these attractors, the model then said this: All actions come from beliefs. These beliefs result from programs. The programs come from early experiences within the driving influences of survival and identity. The programmed behavior flows through filters of our nature and nurture experiences. And those behaviors are attracted toward a state of pleasure and/or peace and/or power.

Figure 4.5, on the next page, shows how attractors fit into our basic programming model.

Let me define what I mean by these attractor terms. And I'll do that in the context of explaining the healthy and unhealthy ways to fulfill these needs. Pleasure is the abiding joy and gratitude you can experience in life. It is manifested in being happy, having fun and having a sense of humor. This is the healthy way to possess and experience the state of pleasure.

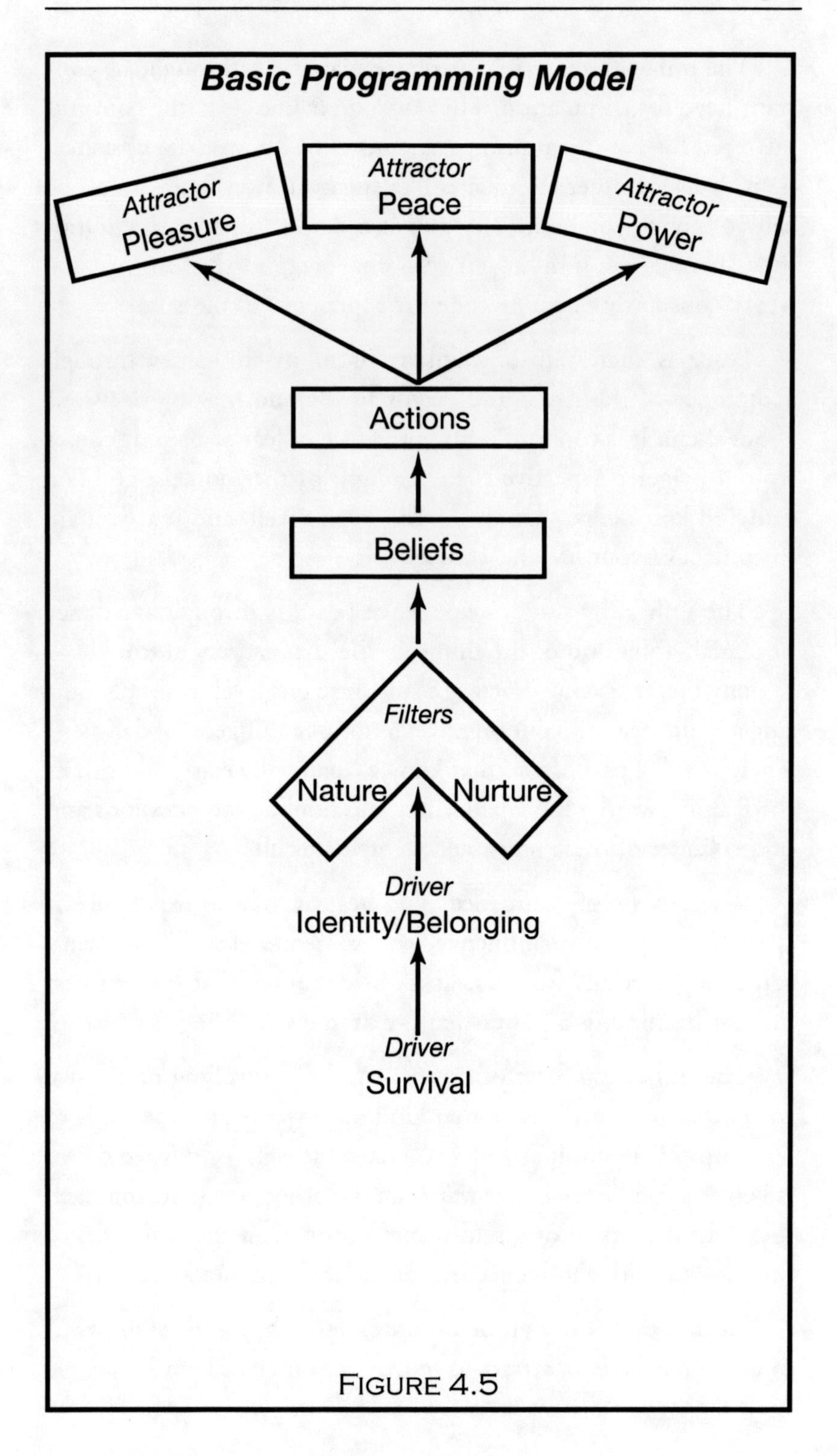
Basic Programming Model
Attractor
Pleasure
Attractor
Peace
Attractor
Power
Actions
Beliefs
Filters
Nature
Nurture
Driver
Identity/Belonging
Driver
Survival

FIGURE 4.5

The unhealthy way to experience pleasure is through the constant need for stimulation. The next adrenaline rush, the continuous need for new relationships, the next "fix" from that substance, be it drugs or other stimulants like sugar or even food can all be ways of giving you temporary pleasure. And this temporary fulfillment is not very fulfilling. It feels shallow, and you can become weary constantly pursuing the next experience of pleasure.

Peace is that state of calm or harmony. It comes through acceptance of the issues and events in life and making decisions about them. It is constant even in the face of fear or pain. It comes from a bigger perspective than the light of the moment and is a centered knowledge that all is well, will be well, and that you are in control of your life and choices.

The unhealthy way to experience peace is through avoidance or denial. To get rid of the things in life that cause you trouble or to deny their existence, even at a subconscious level, is simply putting a white coat of paint on the exterior of a dungeon of darkness. There is still a part of you that knows what really exists and carries the fear and worry, the anxiousness and doubts, the questions and uncertainties of these unwanted elements of life.

Power is simply influence. The healthy way to experience it is to have a positive influence over someone else. To influence someone, especially from a heart of love that has that person's best interest in mind, is a power that is extremely fulfilling.

The unhealthy form of power is to be controlling or abusive to another person. To have that kind of power over someone is to "over power" them. It assumes you have the right or duty to do so. It believes you have a better way than the other person to approach life. And it is more of a selfish interaction than the real form of power—a positive influence that is selfless in nature.

Notice, these three attractors are states of being. Each draws us but one, maybe two, attract us more than others. There are people who have come to our Personal Growth Intensive who are out for joy in everything they do. Fun, happiness and gratitude is an everyday state of being no matter what is being done. Others have had that constant attraction of a peace-filled existence. They have a marvelous method of accepting life and engaging in harmony with what surrounds them.

Joann and I find that power—the positive influence from selfless love—is the attractor that has the most draw to us. We have often said, "Our highest joy is making a positive difference in someone's life!"

Notice the interesting irony? When we have that kind of influence it causes us joy as a natural result. And when we walk away from an experience that has truly made a powerful difference in someone else's life, that joy is translated into a sense of deep and fulfilling peace. These attractors do, indeed, interplay.

These attractors don't have as much power as the drivers nor do they have as much power as the filters. They do have power, however and will affect you depending on your programs within them.

At some point you learned what is important regarding pleasure, peace, and power. These beliefs created programs of behavior associated with those beliefs. So, when you are attracted to pleasure, for instance, your actions and responses will coincide with your "pleasure programs."

At this point I thought I had the model complete. I began testing it by thinking about and observing all kinds of behaviors and responses to see if they found a home in the five areas of the model: Survival, Identity, Nature, Nurture, Pleasure, Peace and Power. Everything fit until, very soon into my search, I sang a song.

"Where does music fit?" I asked myself. "In fact, where do all of the arts fit?" I pondered.

Certainly music, crafts, art—all could be done for pleasure. Some people probably found their identity in one or more of them. But it seemed to be broader and deeper than either of those two observations. As I began looking at humankind in general, I noticed that every culture in the world had these elements as a natural part of life. Whether it was a unique and fantastic gothic cathedral in Europe or a crudely carved stick in an African tribe, all societies had art or craft of some sort. All had music. All had behaviors and traditions that were based on life's courage, struggles or experiences but were not necessarily logical in their consistency of fitting into any of the elements in the model thus far. Further, a person could have or enjoy art without being an artist. Galleries make their money on this fact. A person could enjoy music without being a musician. The recording industry is a multi-billion dollar industry because of this truth, not to mention the radio stations that play the songs.

I watched a National Geographic special about a tribe so deeply secluded in the jungle and so primitive that they had never made contact with a white man before. Even they had art, music, dance, body paint and crafts. Where was this behavior coming from? What need was it fulfilling? How come it didn't neatly fit into any one of the elements of the model so far?

Then I discovered an additional component of the model. In fact, this is one of the areas the seminar group I took to Hawaii helped me fine-tune. And, in reality, closely associated with this finding was one more, and the last, component of the model. These last two components are ***"influencers."***

The elements of art, music, the appreciation of beauty, all fit into the higher form of our being. It comes from our spiritual being. I don't mean religious, I mean ***spiritual***—that part of us that is connected to a deeper, higher and broader existence, power and expression. It is often lived out in religion, but even so called non-religious people still have this sense of cosmic connection and appreciation of beauty.

And I called it an influencer because it influences everything on the model thus far. What you believe about spirituality (or, your "programs" in the area of spirituality) influences how you will experience pleasure, peace and power. It influences how you view your filters and certainly how you live out your identity with your sense of belonging as well as your views about and responses toward survival issues.

A person with no faith or belief about an afterlife may have the program of tenacious self-preservation when it comes to survival—and take down anyone who gets in the way of surviving. A person with a strong belief in a literal and meaningful afterlife may have the program of self-sacrifice, even sacrificing health or life itself, for another person because this life and body are meaningless anyway.

The beliefs or programs in the area of spirituality will influence the other areas of the model in similar ways. A person who believes he or she is a child of God will experience different behavior in the area of identity and belonging than a person who believes he or she exists solely and disconnectedly. Thus spirituality was added to the model as an influencer.

See Figure 4.6 on the next page for how the influencer spirituality fits into our basic programming model.

The spiritual influencer led me to find another influencer. After finding the spiritual one, I asked myself, is there any other deep and broadly based influencer? More research, (and I didn't have to go too far) led me to find the influencer of sexuality. It was not too difficult to see how the sexual drive, appetite, urge, or whatever else you wanted to call it, influences us regularly. And it influences all aspects of the model.

Sexual urges can lead us to procreate, thus our race and legacy survive. Sex can be done for identity or a sense of belonging. It can be pleasurable. It can be used to overpower, empower or to feel

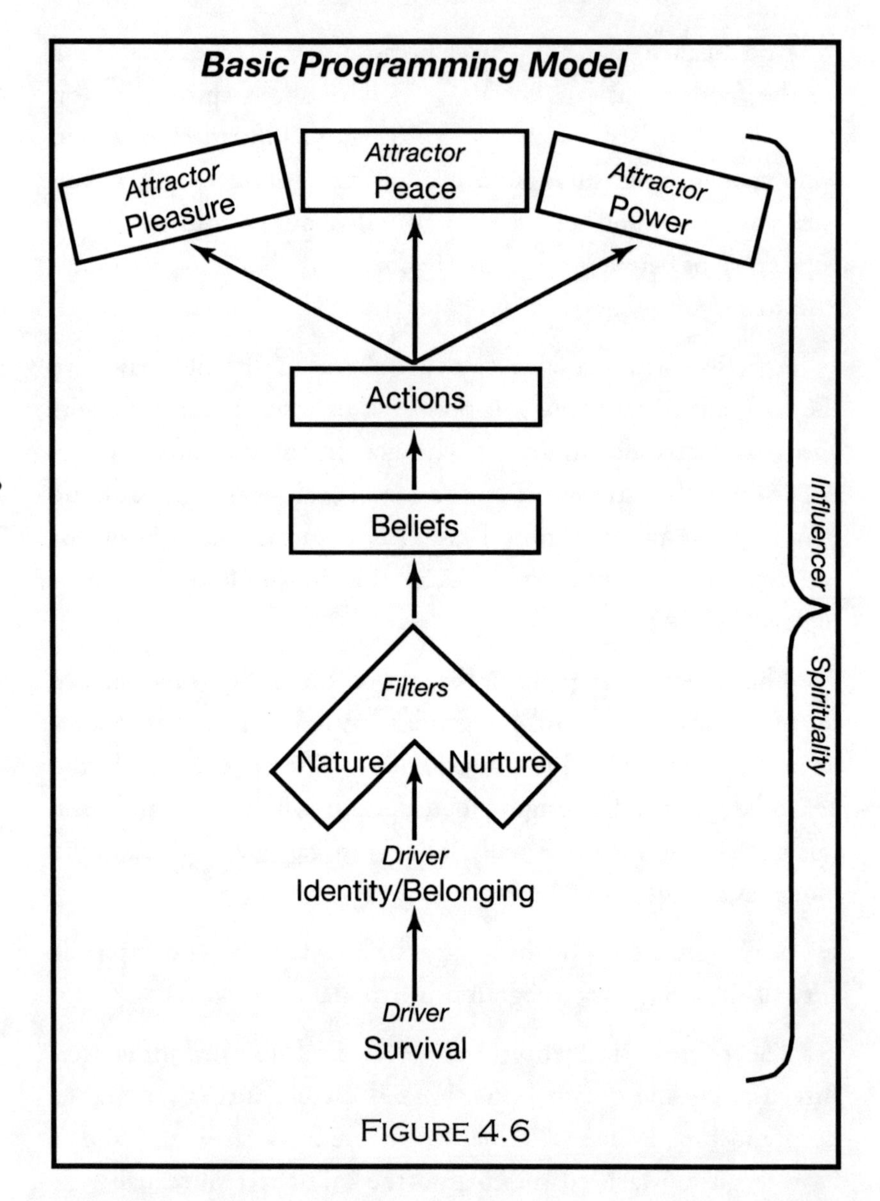

FIGURE 4.6

the power of its force. And the release of sexual energy can bring a great peace.

What you believe about sexuality and the act of sex produces programs that affect ***how*** you engage in the other areas of the model.

The power of these two influencers can be seen in everyday conversation. Engage a person in a conversation about sexuality or spirituality and you have a passionate interchange on your hands. Begin expressing what you believe is right and wrong about these two subject areas and the energy and passion increase.

And remember, your perspectives will be coming from ***your*** beliefs that are the foundation of ***your*** programs. But you will speak with the passion that surrounds your talking about some eternal truth. You've heard the power, right? Aunt Martha telling you what music is good for you and what music is down right bad. Uncle Joe telling you about what art is and what it isn't. Mom telling you what is right and wrong about certain sexual behavior and beliefs while Dad tells you something different.

Truly, spirituality and sexuality are strong influencers of all aspects of our life. And you develop beliefs and programs within these areas, too. How this very important and enjoyable influencer fits in our model can be seen in Figure 4.7 on the next page.

So, that's the model. It claims to explain and predict all human behavior, attitude and response. The theory is this: If you can understand your basic programs in these nine areas (Survival, Identity, Nature, Nurture, Pleasure, Peace, Power, Spirituality and Sexuality) you can understand why you do what you do. You can fully understand yourself. Further, I believe that all experiences in life have dynamics that fit within one or more of these program areas. If this is true, and you understand how your programs work within these nine areas, then you can predict what you will do when you encounter a new experience.

Of course, the fuzzy logic principle in chapter three comes into play here too. All of these programming areas are being considered at the same time. Another way of saying it is that all of the programs are firing at the same time—certainly to a greater or lesser degree depending on the situation. A true survival threat, for

Basic Programming Model

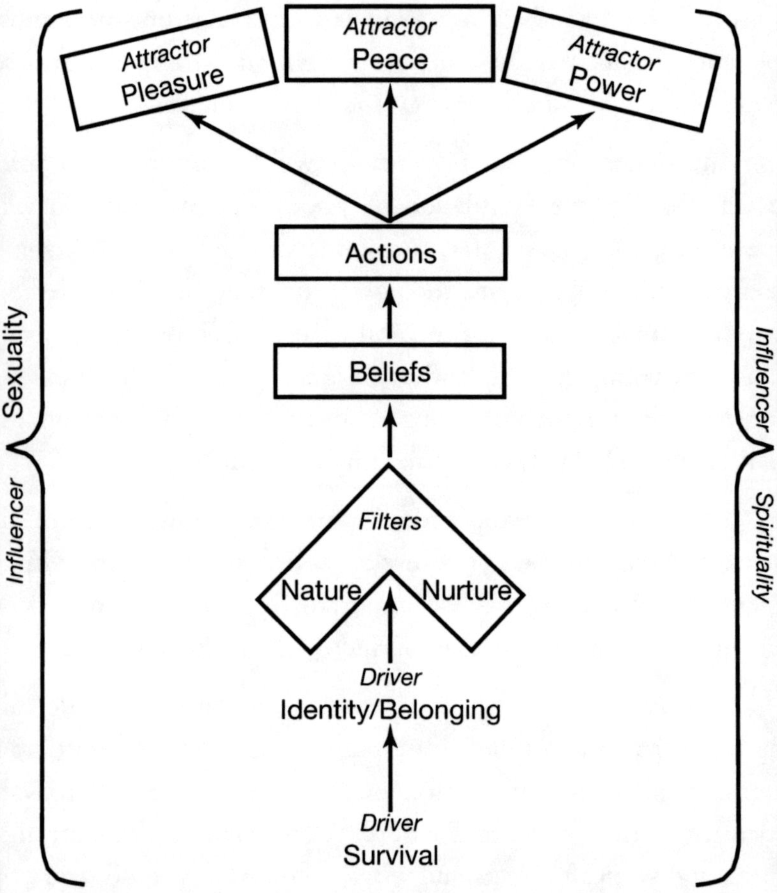

Attractor Pleasure
Attractor Peace
Attractor Power
Actions
Beliefs
Filters
Nature
Nurture
Driver Identity/Belonging
Driver Survival
Sexuality
Influencer
Influencer
Spirituality

FIGURE 4.7

example, may engage the spiritual and survival programs. Someone flirting with you may invoke the sexual and identity programs, and possibly the pleasure and/or power programs too. Nevertheless, understanding your programs, what types of dynamics would cause them to fire, and how they interact, will enable you to predict your behavior in any given situation.

This concept is freeing and not fatalistic. I am ***not*** saying you are stuck in this cause and effect dance. However, you will be unless you consciously choose to change. Until then, you are simply a product of your past (as per our chapter two principle). But when you become aware of your programs and make choices about them, they are no longer in control of you. You are in control of them.

And that is what we will deal with specifically in chapter six. We will show you how to find your programs and give you three ways to manage or change them.

What is the reason for waiting for chapter six and not doing it in the next chapter, chapter five?

There is an incredible set of beliefs and programs nearly universally held within the concepts of identity and belonging. Invariably we find people need to understand the concepts embedded in this area before they can feel free enough to find and deal with their other programs.

Actually, I have been teaching the concepts of the next chapter for the past twenty-five years (as of this writing) and have had fascinating consistency in regards to people's awareness, understandings and needs in the concepts of identity and belonging. In the next chapter you will learn how to have a confident, healthy self-esteem, how to experience freedom from someone else's control, and how to have a sense of personal power.

Joann will rejoin me in the next chapter. And if you are anything like the thousands of people we have taught over the years, I can't wait for you to read the next chapter because I can anticipate the end of your story. The benefits and freedom you will sense from learning about the concepts in this area are...well...I'll save my excitement and just let you read the words.

Chapter 5

How to Have a Healthy Self-Esteem ...Developing Confidence and Personal Power!

John could be in a room full of people and still feel lonely. It didn't matter if he was at a party with friends or with a crowd of strangers. If he stopped for just a moment and did a check-in with his inner self, he would feel hollow and empty. His inner voice was filled with doubt and longings for love. He wanted to be accepted and fit in.

To others, this need for acceptance didn't really make any sense. He had everything going for him. He had no enemies. From other people's perspectives he was popular and loved. If asked, others would emphatically tell you how John fit in wherever he went. In fact, if he was with a group of people he was meeting for the first time, it wouldn't take long before he was not just a part of the party, he was the life of the party. Others would willingly engage with him, talk with him, laugh at his jokes, and be genuinely interested in his life. They were impressed with John. But all of this didn't satisfy him. It didn't fulfill his deepest felt need. He was lonely, though rarely ever alone.

How can this happen? What can cause such a difference between inner and outer experience? How can people say one thing about John and he believe and experience something so different?

If you think that is strange, listen to this paradox: Another person, Sally, who was very different from John, could look at him and wish she had what he had. Indeed, from her perspective he had exactly what she was looking for to satisfy her inner need, her need to be accepted, to be loved, to belong and fit in. Notice? That's exactly what John was feeling inside too.

Unlike John, the pogo-stick, bouncing from person to person, conversation to conversation, Sally was just the opposite. She would sit in the corner and engage in conversation with one person for a long time. She would find the depth of meaning in that person's life as it unfolded in intimate detail. Where John was the butterfly, she was the caterpillar. Yet both had the same inner desire and need. No amount of external interaction would satisfy their internal need.

Our external experience and actions can be very convincing, even to ourselves. Yet how we are acting is simply a way of coping, a way to try and meet the inner "driver need" we talked about in the last chapter, the need of identity and belonging. And everyone has this need while very few—extremely few—have found an effective, peace-filled way of fulfilling it. Instead they just keep amplifying their coping behaviors to get by, while on the inside they remain hollow and empty. Confidence is varied. Self-esteem rises and falls with the tide of circumstance.

There are many manifestations of external behavior that come from this consistently similar need. We have spoken about the social butterfly trying to connect with others through swift and entertaining touches. We have talked about the slow moving but meaningful caterpillar who tries to connect by diving deeply into another person's need and perspective. There is another common way people cope, that is by trying too hard.

You have probably seen the person who is always trying to please or always trying to perform. This person loses all sense of self. Others determine what should be done or believed for acceptance. This kind of coping mechanism tries hard to live up to the current social standard and expectation.

This kind of coping behavior cannot usually stand the test of time, however. Eventually the person appears to be a fake or, at least, insincere or disingenuous. People have a hard time relating to this kind of person over time. At first there is praise which is soon replaced with question and finally settled into criticism. These are just three ways people use out of the many ways possible to cope with and try to gain fulfillment for their inner need of identity and belonging. But they don't work. And if they do it is temporary.

We have found that entire audiences of people are able to intimately relate to what we are talking about here. They are weary of working toward the illusive goal of an accepting relationship. They try hard to please their boss, gain love from their spouse and fit in with their friends. But no matter how hard they try or what they do they all seem to stand equal in want and need, all with similar inner experience, all wanting the same fulfillment, the same remedy, the same cure. We are closer companions than most people think.

If you are like most people you can relate to what we are saying. Somehow, this book found its way into your hands and you are reading it with a degree of interest and probably relating at some level to the need we are talking about now. And, based on the previous chapters, you are aware of how you got to be here—previous programs resulting in learned behavior to satisfy inner needs. Now you want to be free.

Stay persistent and we'll help you become free and fulfilled. You will find a solution that will undoubtedly increase your inner peace and happiness. You will feel fulfilled, secure and confident with a healthy dose of personal power. Further, the solution we are talking about in this chapter will make your relationships better, even from the other person's perspective.

Sometimes a person is being driven by their survival programs so their identity and belonging program is waiting in line to be fulfilled. This would be the case in a country where starvation is the rule. It would be the case if you are in a situation where you can't pay your bills and you are in danger of losing the basic necessities of life. You are feeling the weight of responsibility for those who depend on you. You are in imminent danger of losing the survival necessities of food, clothing or shelter.

If survival is at stake you don't care about fitting in or being loved. If you are dying of thirst in the desert and someone finds you, their gentle words of affection or acceptance will be smothered by your cries for water.

In the next chapter you will learn more about how to find your programs in all of the areas of our basic programming model. You will also learn how to manage and reprogram them if you want to. It has been our experience, however, that ***most*** people have their most potent programs operating and driving them in the area of identity and belonging. That is why we are dedicating an entire chapter to this subject. When we have taught people the concepts in this chapter, they gain an immediate sense of release and freedom. They build a wonderful foundation of peace and a stable, powerful confidence.

So let's learn the concepts.

When you are born, you begin relating to what we call a Dominant Parental Influence (DPI). This is not a domineering parent. Rather, it is the most dominant parental influence in your life. It could be Mother or Father. It could be Grandmother or Grandfather. It could even be an older brother or sister. And in some cases, it can even be someone outside your family unit.

This DPI is the person who taught you the meanings about relationship, about identity and about belonging. Figure 5.1 shows this relationship schematically.

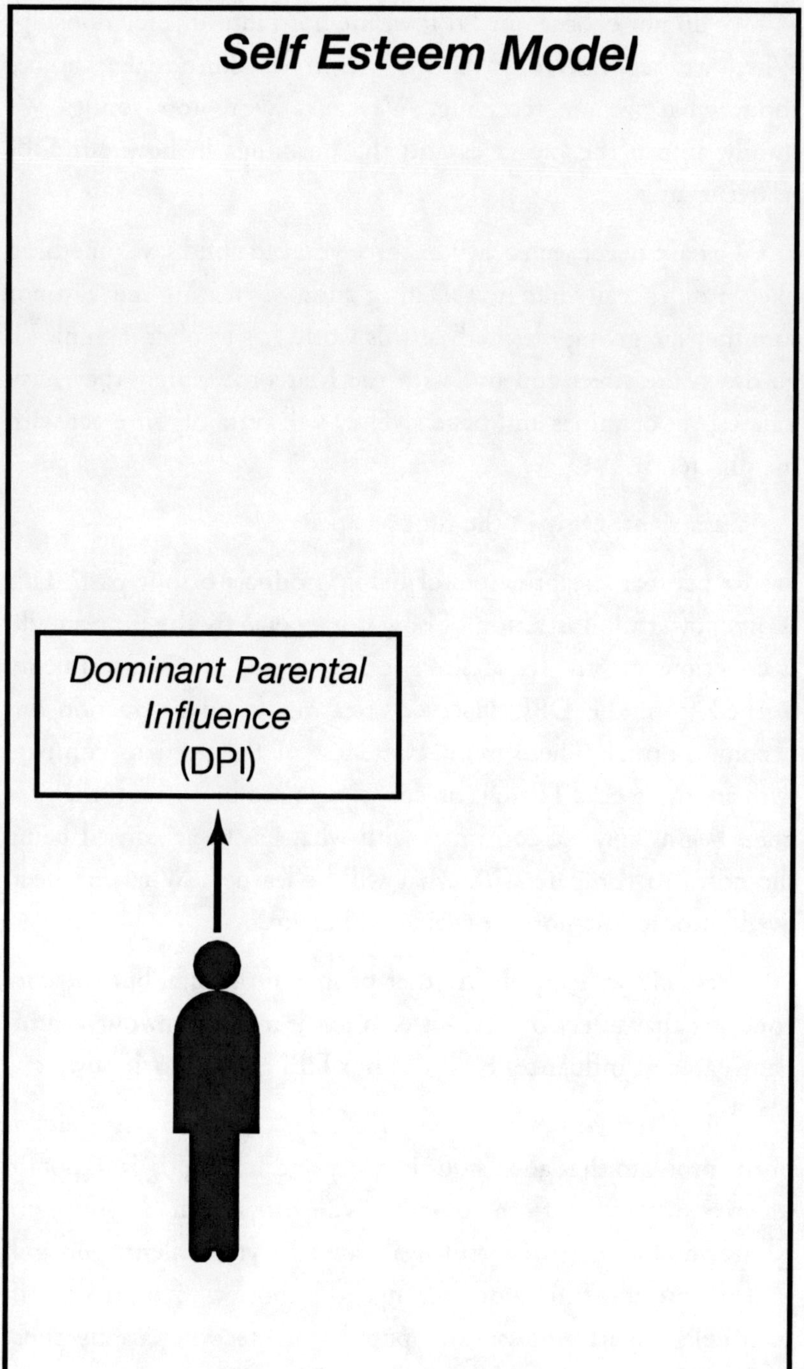

Self Esteem Model

Dominant Parental Influence (DPI)

FIGURE 5.1

We do not choose our DPI; we are born into this relationship. When we begin relating to this person we don't make choices about what we are receiving. We can't. We're too young. We simply absorb the messages and the meanings in how our DPI relates to us.

We have never seen a two or three year old child say something like, "I don't really like how Dad or Mom is treating me. I'm not sure they are giving me the best this world has to offer. I think I'll go down the street and live with the Marconi's, surely they have a better set of values and beliefs. They will certainly interact with me differently."

Yeah, right. Only in the funny papers.

Remember the principle of being products of our past? This is one powerful illustration of how it happens. By the time a child is conscious of how he or she is being treated and what is being learned from the DPI, that very treatment and interaction has become normal. There is no awareness of the need to compare with anything else. There is no conscious need to. Instead, the program begins and life continues with what has been learned being the norm to compare with what will be learned. What has been lived becomes the norm for what will be lived.

Certainly we learn from other people in our life, but the core concepts that affect our self-esteem are learned from our Dominant Parental Influence. How did our DPI get so much power?

The power comes from our need. The core, driving element of the program that affects our identity and belonging is to obtain identity or validity from someone who can give it. If you are a painter and want to be truly validated in your talent, you will find the greatest validation coming from those who are famous in your field. An art professor or a popular painter will have the most impact on you as you seek validation. It's nice to have your peers acknowledge you and it is wonderful to have the non-painting public give you accolades. But the deepest, most powerful validation will come from the masters.

Further, if your peers and the public differ from what the masters say about your painting, at your deepest level, it is the master who determines your "painting-esteem." Your greatest sense of belonging will come from being accepted and associated with those greats. This will mean more to you than accepting words from your peers or your public.

To be clear, we acknowledge how good it may feel for your peers to praise you, and how lucrative it can be to have the public demand your work. But those fill different needs. The core need for validity, acceptance and belonging will be most effectively fulfilled by those to whom you look to fulfill that need. And, contrasting that, this will be the same entity to whom you look to learn what to avoid so as not to be rejected.

One more example: At work, if your fellow worker says, "You're fired," it has no impact. It is only your supervisor to whom you look to for acceptance, validation, or potential rejection who has that power. In your family, siblings or the less powerful parental figure would have less influence on you. Only the person who possesses the power of the DPI role can affect your core needs regarding acceptance, identity and belonging. You, therefore, look to the person with the greatest potential and power for acceptance and rejection to give you ***your*** sense of acceptance or rejection.

So, who is your Dominant Parental Influence?

You would not be accurate by saying it is always the mother or the father, or it is always the older one or even the louder or more the one with greater physical or personality strength. Your DPI is not determined by these kinds of manifestations. Nor is it determined by role. It is relationship based.

Your DPI is the person to whom you look for acceptance; it can even be a deceased parent whose relationship is kept alive by the living parent. Let's say, for example, that your father died when you were very young, or even before your birth. Mom's constant message of, "I'm glad your father is not alive to see that," or "What would your father say if he saw you doing that," or even, "Remember, your father is watching everything you are doing." If this happens, you begin to calibrate your actions on what your father ***would have*** said or done as interpreted and perpetuated by your mother.

Also, your DPI is not necessarily the person you spent most of your time with. You may have spent most of your time with your mother, but your father possessed the greatest influence in setting the standards for acceptance and rejection. This can be amplified, supported and perpetuated by your mother deferring to your rarely present father. This is done with phrases like "Wait until your father gets home," or "Wait until I tell your father about that," or even, "You know I can't decide that; I'll ask your father."

Let's be clear about something at this point. We are talking about *acceptance and belonging*. We are not talking about being loved. You may know you are loved, but you become "unacceptable" if you don't behave. You may ***know*** you are loved, but you don't ***feel*** loved. We'll amplify this more later. For now, as you focus on this concept, know that you are exploring being *accepted*, not being loved.

Most people know who their DPI is. Some aren't sure. And, indeed, sometimes it is ***both*** parents, but most of the time it is one person. Here are a few explorative questions you can ask yourself to help you determine your DPI. No one question is more important than another, and you may not be able to relate to all questions. As you look at this list of questions as a whole, it can help you get a good indication of who your DPI is. Try to answer each question with the first thing that comes to your mind. Do it before reading the brief description after the question.

1. *Who was the head of the house?*

   The concept of being the "head of the house" can vary in meaning for different people. Think of it from *your* perspective as well as what other people might say about your family unit.

2. *From whom did you ask permission to do things?*

   Often there is one person who needs to make all the decisions. In fact to ask the other person is a waste of time. You, or the parent you are asking, would still need to ask the decision maker anyway.

3. *If you asked your parents for permission to do something and Mother said, "yes" while Father said, "no," who would win?*

   The person who consistently won the arguments might be a clue as to who had the most power of influence in the relationship.

4. *Who "wore the pants" in your family?*

   This is a strange question for some people, but there are many people, especially from the "old school," who seem to relate to it.

5. *If someone outside your family structure wanted your family to go on an outing, whom would they ask?*

   This is a question that, once again, looks for the power structure, the person everyone looked to for direction and decision.

6. *Whom did you feel you needed acceptance from more than anyone else?*

   Regardless of what you did or how many other people gave you words of support or acceptance, which parental figure did you want to accept you? This is the figure that would be analogous to the painting masters in the illustration above.

7. *When you performed a major accomplishment, whom were you most anxious to tell?*

   Typically, a child is happy to have various people know about a major accomplishment. It even feels good to have aunts and uncles know and praise. But the one person you crave to know about it is your DPI. It is this very accomplishment you hope will give you a greater degree of acceptance.

8. *How did you relate to being disciplined when you did something wrong?*

   The most potent time for teaching and learning a standard of acceptance is during discipline. The question, then, has more to do with how you viewed discipline not necessarily who did it. What were the messages that surrounded discipline? Were you a "bad person" because of what you did or were you a person who did a "bad thing?" And whose words, messages, meanings were more important to you when it came to being disciplined? If Dad gave you a "time out" did it mean the same and have the same effect as if Mom did it?

Let's say a bit more about discipline. This is one of the most potent times when we learn the messages of acceptance or rejection. This is an extremely powerful moment. It's because we already know, or have been told, that we have done something wrong. If our acceptance is based on performance, we are already behind the proverbial 8-ball. In fact, we expect rejection. If the message we receive during discipline is lack of acceptance that amplifies what we are already telling ourselves. This effectively doubles the power of the message.

To prove the power of the message associated with discipline, consider this: Your DPI tells you how wonderful you are and how accepted you are—for 100 days in a row. On the 101st day you do something wrong and you here told, "You good for nothing $#@%$#@! You will never amount to anything!" Then, for the next 100 days you hear the message of love and acceptance. "I love you. I'm happy you are my child. You are great!"

201 days of messages. 200 of the messages are accepting, 1 rejecting. Which one are you going to remember? Invariably people say the day of rejection. How discipline is handled becomes a major contributor toward our belief systems regarding conditional or unconditional acceptance.

The answers to the above questions can help you understand who your Dominant Parental Influence was. When you identify your DPI remember this: we are ***not blaming*** them for anything! And you should not either. Parents, too, are making the best choices available to them. (Remember the principle?) Even if your parent was overtly destructive, the same principles you have learned in this book apply to them as much as they apply to you. That parent is simply living out learned programs too.

So, we are not blaming, we are simply understanding. We have seen situations where it is extremely obvious that a person is living out a reactive life based on what they learned from their DPI. One man, Jack, who came to our Personal Growth Intensive, was obviously distant, attacking, and manipulative. (And we could say more). It didn't take long at all to see where it was coming from.

Jack's father—Jack's DPI—was a high-ranking military man with characteristics similar to Jack's. Jack wanted acceptance from his father. He tried to gain that acceptance by being like his father. But it never worked. Further analysis revealed that Jack's father was living out a life of trying to get acceptance from ***his*** father. And the grain in the wood from the family tree goes on.

Even though Jack could understand the origin of his behavior, how it played into his self-esteem, and how he was trying to get acceptance from everyone, his place was *not* to understand and then wallow in the wasteland of blame. His place was to understand and make a choice about what he wanted for his life. Because he accepted this important principle, he had the privilege of stopping the chain of reactive living in his becoming free.

The issue is to ***understand*** who your DPI is, not to blame. This understanding gives you a focal point for further exploration about this subject. As you focus on your DPI, you can begin asking the question, "What did I learn from my Dominant Parental Influence?"

As you ask that question, you may discover a variety of things you have learned. You may find out why you like certain kinds of food, clothes or activities. You may discover why you behave in certain ways in certain situations—always shying away from public gatherings, for example, because your DPI taught you it was unsafe.

Regardless of what you learned about behaviors, beliefs and values, there is one basic concept everyone learns from their Dominant Parental Influence, and that is a *standard of acceptance,* what makes us acceptable or not.

This standard of acceptance takes on one of two forms: Conditional Acceptance or Unconditional Acceptance. Examine Figure 5.2 on the next page, and then we will explain these terms.

The standard of acceptance is simply the basic beliefs we develop regarding what makes us acceptable or not. We learn this unconsciously at an early age. Through word and action, our Dominant Parental Influence teaches us what is acceptable and what is not. The DPI does this through what is said and the attitude with which it is spoken. Wrinkling the nose, snarling and talking with a harsh tone about what someone else has said or done teaches the observer what the DPI thinks about the issue—even if the observer is a young child. Obvious actions are quick teachers. A slap or a yell associated with something the child does can give the obvious message of "rejection."

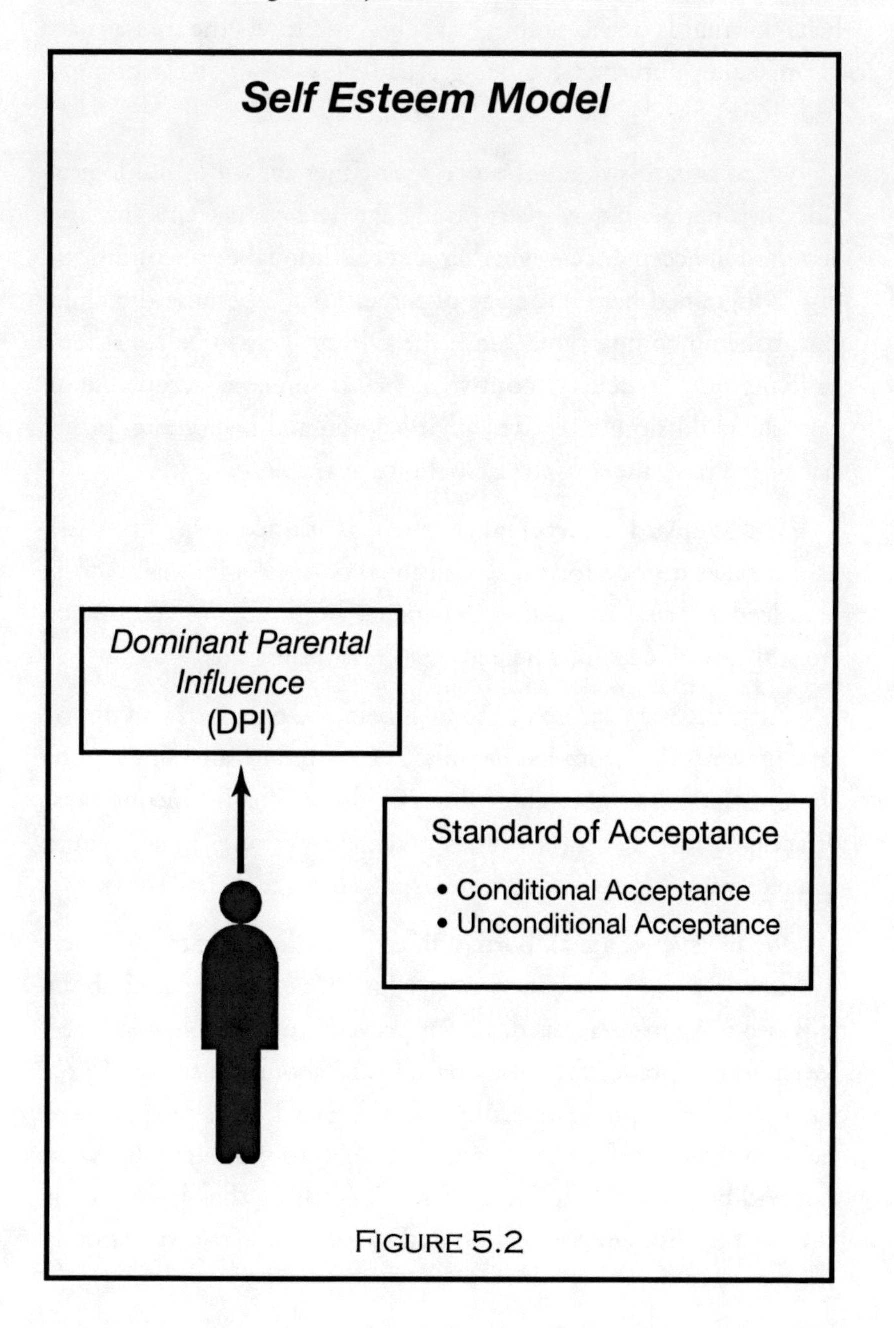

FIGURE 5.2

Unfortunately a child doesn't have the capacity to make the distinction between behavior and person. When a DPI punishes the child for a certain behavior, if that punishment is not associated with overt word and action that says, "I accept ***you***, it is the behavior that is unacceptable," the child interprets the message as, "I am being punished for being a bad ***person***," (not for doing a bad thing).

Of course, this thought process is neither conscious nor logical since it is happening at a very young age. In fact, it seems that the standard of acceptance—whether it is conditional or unconditional—is ingrained before the age of three. That is because the child can make no comparisons. Since the DPI is likely to be consistent in living out the beliefs about what makes someone acceptable or not, the child simply receives what is given and becomes a "product of the past, making the best choice available."

The standard of acceptance, then, is learned at a very early age. It takes on two forms: Conditional or Unconditional. And it is indeed an "or." You *cannot* experience both types of acceptance from the same person. There are two reasons for this.

First, the very nature of the two, being so polarized and opposite, prevents that from happening. The second reason comes from the illustration we gave about the 201 days. When someone says, "I accept you," then says with as much conviction, "I reject you," the receiver of these two comments has to make a choice.

We believe we are all born with the need for acceptance which indicates we don't have it to start with. If we were neutral about this, we wouldn't crave it. It's been proven, however, that we need love and acceptance. You may have heard about the study of premature infants whose mortality rate decreased because they were being touched and held by nurses than those infants who were not. Additionally, there are a variety of studies that have shown the need for human connection and validation. Maslowe's famous hierarchy of needs proved that after safety and physiological needs were fulfilled, we have the need for love and belonging.

But there is no need to cite the studies. We have been teaching this subject for many years. Everyone has seen this fact as a self-evident truth. No one argues with the need to be loved, validated, and accepted. No one argues with our innate need to belong. So the argument is logical. If we sense the need for acceptance, it's because we don't have it in the first place. Somehow, when we are born, we are born with this need for identity and belonging.

It's like our need for oxygen. Because we need it, when we are deprived of it, we immediately sense the need, a desperate need, for air. If we didn't need it and were deprived of it, we may desire it but it wouldn't be a driving need.

So, if we get the above two messages, one that speaks of acceptance and one that speaks equally of rejection, as a child we are going to default to the one that aligns with the belief we already have, that is, not being accepted while still needing it. Further, we will take the dynamics of whatever it is that surrounds the message and extrapolate them into our belief and experience. If we get scolded for talking too loudly in the store, we interpret that by saying to our self, "I am a bad person for talking too loudly in the store." And that thought is accompanied with the antithesis thought, "To be accepted, I must not do something bad like talk too loudly in the store." And this is how we build the implementation belief systems surrounding our basic belief system of conditional or unconditional acceptance.

The above illustration speaks to building the belief system of *conditional acceptance.* Here is how it works with *unconditional acceptance.*

If Tommy talks too loudly in the store, an unconditionally accepting DPI will make the distinction between behavior and person and say something like this, "Tommy, stop talking so loudly in the store. You are a great person and I love you, son. But what you are doing has to change. It is unacceptable." Notice, the ***behavior*** is unacceptable, not the person. And this message, though it may be worded differently, is consistent with what Tommy always hears – that is a separation of person from behavior.

It is time to be clear about the difference between conditional and unconditional acceptance.

Conditional acceptance is performance based. It is acceptance based on what you do, not based on who you are. Acceptance comes from how well you behave, act or perform. What you do determines who you are.

Unconditional acceptance distinguishes between the person and the behavior. The person is always unconditionally accepted and the behavior is held separately. What you do flows from who you are but does not determine who you are. With unconditional acceptance you have inherent value and worth as a person. Decisions about behavior, actions, and performance are made separately.

Unconditional acceptance does not say, "Anything goes." Appropriate responses, everything from praise to criticism, from freedom to restraint, from like to dislike—are all made about what the person is doing, not about the person.

Naturally, you make choices about how you are going to relate to the person based on their actions, but you know that the person has value and worth simply because he or she is another human being. You defend yourself against a person who is attacking you. You avoid a person who is offensive. And, yes, these are extreme cases, but the principle remains true. Unconditional acceptance always accepts the person ***and*** makes a decision about how to relate to that person based upon behavior.

The distinction is simple but has profound effects. A conditionally accepting DPI gives the message that you can only be accepted if you perform well or behave "correctly." An unconditionally accepting DPI gives the message of acceptance to the child as a person then guides, praises, teaches or disciplines the child regarding behavior. The key is this, the unconditionally accepting DPI always communicates a clear and overt distinction between behavior and person.

The conditionally accepting DPI would say, "Go to your room until you can be a better person." The unconditionally accepting DPI would say, "Go to your room. I accept you, but what you are doing is unacceptable. You can come out when you choose to behave appropriately." In the first case, what you do determines who you are. In the second, what you do results from who you are.

There is a subtle yet powerful truth that is embedded in these two philosophies. When you believe that what you do determines who you are and your acceptance in life, you are constantly focused on behavior to create or correct your identity. It is a helpless stance. You become a victim of your behavior, your habits, your performance. You are not in control. You are constantly looking around for the standards of behavior that, if followed, make you acceptable. You are constantly trying to do the right behaviors that make you OK.

When you believe that what you do flows from who you are instead of determining who you are, your behavior becomes an indicator not a dictator. You can look at what you have done, like it or not like it, receive that input, then make choices about how you will behave next time. With this belief system, you ***are*** in control. You are freer to adjust your behavior because your choices aren't limited to someone else's determinates: "If you do 'this' you are acceptable.

Which do you think most of us grow up with? When we have asked that question to thousands of people in seminars around the country the answer is consistent and obvious, "Conditional acceptance." It seems to be rare to find someone who has been raised with unconditional acceptance. We have theories about why this is, but that is beyond the scope of this book. The theories notwithstanding, the fact remains that nearly everyone we have asked claims to have been raised with conditional acceptance.

Some people are confused at first because they lived up to all the standards laid out for them. In other words, they thought they had unconditional acceptance simply because they never had any problems. In reality, they were simply very proficient at doing the right things so their DPI gave them acceptance. The key is this, they got their acceptance for what they did, not for who they were.

As we talk with these individuals we would ask them questions about what would have happened if they disobeyed or rebelled. The response was something like, "But I never did." As we persist in this thought experiment, they acknowledge that if they didn't do everything right, there would have been problems with their DPI. They verbalize problems that sound like conditional acceptance: "My 'DPI' wouldn't have liked me very much," or "My DPI would have a real problem with ***me***," or other words that indicate conditional acceptance. Potential rejection is synonymous with conditional acceptance.

True unconditional acceptance manifests itself in the knowledge and belief that there is nothing you can do that would cause your DPI to reject you. Though the DPI may be disappointed—or even get the authorities to restrain you for your violent—there would still be acceptance of you as a person.

As you grow up and experience new relationships in life and new venues of interaction, your original belief about your standard of acceptance becomes stronger. It is amplified by the dynamics of school, work, play, etc.

When you go to school you periodically get report cards. Children with a conditional acceptance standard see the grades as what determines their value. Bad grades mean bad person. The report card gets lost, hidden or in some way justified to make sure there isn't an undue amount of rejecting words or actions from the DPI.

The students with the standard of unconditional acceptance see the grades as an indicator of how they did, not who they are. The grades give helpful input as to what the student needs to do to obtain a desired grade.

The same dynamics occur when you go to work or play in sports. Evaluations or coaching input is seen by the conditionally accepted person as judgment. It is tortuous. The unconditionally accepted person can even welcome the evaluation or coaching. It is a chance to get feedback for improvement. To the conditionally accepted person, input is a hammer or a hug. To the unconditionally accepted person, input is simply a mirror.

Behavior that comes from an unconditionally accepting person is without baggage; it is without hidden agenda, and it is without meaning of acceptance or rejection. Behavior that comes from a conditionally accepting person is almost always manifested in one of two forms: Excelling or Rebelling.

Our first instinct is to "excel," to try and live up to the standard of acceptance we encounter so we can be accepted. Excelling behavior is when you are trying to live up to the expectations of another person, or even of yourself. Approval for the level of performance is interpreted as acceptance. Acceptance, then, is experienced at the level of performance achieved. The more successful the performance, the more acceptance you feel. The feelings of acceptance fluctuate with the level of accomplishment, but no matter how great the accomplishment, it will not satisfy the inner craving for acceptance on a deeper level.

If acceptance does not occur when we make an attempt to excel, we may rebel so we can, at least, get some attention from that. Strangely enough, our subconscious mind translates any attention as a form of acceptance. "They care enough to get involved." Also, attention gives a form of connection with another person, even if it is a negative connection. Further, rebelling can give a person a form of identity.

Rebelling behavior is when you go against the expectations of the authority to whom you are relating at the moment. This allows you to get some attention. This attention, though negative in nature, is interpreted as a form of acceptance. The level of attention you receive, however, only acts as a temporary pacifier for the *inner craving of unconditional acceptance.*

Since most of us are raised with conditional acceptance, an unfortunate time this is manifested is when we become attracted to and develop a relationship with someone we want to be committed to.

Remember the principles that speak to our being products of our past, making the best choice available to us, and living out the dynamics of our past? Notice how these play out with a conditionally accepted person. Let's use Mark as an example.

Mark is born with the need for acceptance and learns that to get it, he has to have good behavior. He grows up, all the while wanting to be accepted and trying to get that acceptance through his performance in school, work and life in general. Who is he trying to get acceptance from? Obviously, from his DPI. So, as he goes through life, he lives out the dynamics of his past. The teacher, then, to his subconscious mind, is not his teacher; it is Mark's DPI. His employer is his DPI.

Let's amplify this a bit more. Another way of saying that we live out the dynamics of our past is to say, "We can only relate in relation to the relationships we have known." So, when we interact with someone, we can only "position them," so to speak, in the positions that are available to us.

The conditionally accepted person only has the positions available of DPI and child. Because of past dynamics and inner need, the conditionally accepted person goes through life wanting a "DPI" to give acceptance. For example, Mark would initially look up to anyone he met as a potential DPI who could give him acceptance. If that didn't happen, the only other dynamic he had learned, the only other "position" available to him, was that of child, so Mark becomes the DPI to this person in the relationship.

The unconditionally accepted person has three positions available, that of parent, child and equal. When the child grows up, the unconditionally accepting DPI continues to give acceptance even though the child (an adult now) may differ in beliefs, values or behavior. The message is that it is ok to be an equal with differences. This allows for the third position of equality that will be lived out with most people in life.

So, continuing with Mark's example, if he had conditional acceptance growing up and is attracted to Amber, who is Amber to him? Because of the dynamics of his past—because he can only relate in relation to the relationships he has known, because he is making the best choice available to him—Mark initially looks to Amber as his DPI. He longs for her to give him acceptance.

If Amber grew up with conditional acceptance, and that is likely, who is Mark to her? Right! Mark is her DPI. So they are looking to each other to fill an inner need that is inappropriate to fill—that of being the other person's parent.

We have seen so many relationships with problems that stem from this core dynamic. Over time, Mark and Amber may gravitate towards having continued conflict or settle into working roles. One of them may live in the child role and the other in the DPI role. But that is not very fulfilling for either of them over the long run.

There is hope, however. We have seen many people be freed from this dynamic and have more fulfilling relationships. That is what this book is all about, becoming free and letting what you do flow from the wonderful person you are. More on that as we move forward.

As you analyze this issue more completely, you notice what is happening. Based on all the principles you have already learned you can undoubtedly see how your view of self, (your self-esteem, how you "esteem yourself") is learned from your DPI. Further, the perspective and dynamics of the relationship are projected onto other relationships you encounter.

Anytime you relate to an authority figure, you relate to them with the same dynamics you learned from your initial authority figure, your DPI. This occurs because of the laws of life (the principles you learned in the second chapter): You are a product of your past, you live out the same dynamics of you past if you encounter a situation that parallels those dynamics, you place meaning on what you are experiencing based on your past, and you make the best choice available to you;—in short, you can only relate in relation to the relationships you have known (unless you become aware of the problem and *consciously choose to change*).

Any person that you look up to falls prey to your DPI dynamic. If you are interacting with a patrolman, a judge, a teacher, a boss, or even someone you look up to as an authority of any kind—you are subconsciously relating to your DPI, not the person present and you try to gain their acceptance or approval by your actions and performance. Superimposed on their body is a subconscious projection of the image and interaction of your DPI. When you get a speeding ticket, it is not the patrolman giving you the ticket, it is your DPI catching you doing something wrong and punishing you. Notice how it looks in the diagram on the next page (Figure 5.3).

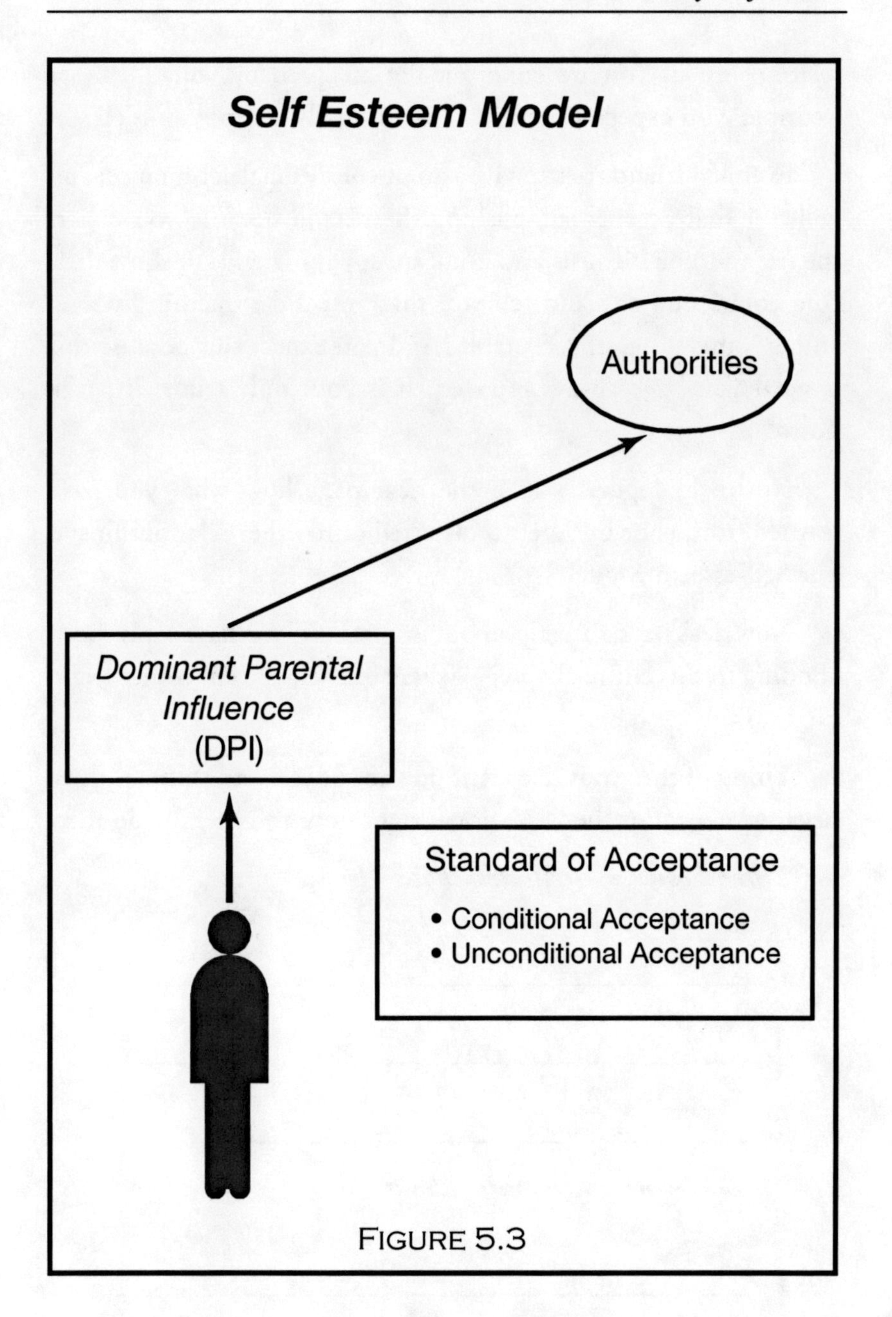

FIGURE 5.3

You also project the dynamics of your DPI relationship onto others you interact with that are not authority figures. You expect, however, the same kind of relationship as what exists in your DPI relationship. If you are conditionally accepted by your DPI, for example, you expect a friend to conditionally accept you too.

Even if a friend tries to give you unconditional acceptance, you will test that acceptance, pushing the person because you ***expect*** the friend to be inconsistent. You expect your friends to show their true colors one day and tell you that you did something wrong and are, therefore, unacceptable. And you expect this because this is what you have always received. It is your only truth. It is the norm.

Notice in Figure 5.4 on the next page how what you have learned from your DPI gets transferred onto other relationships in our Self-esteem Model.

Now let's talk directly about something we have only been alluding to this entire chapter—where our self-esteem comes from. First do this exercise.

Think of three positive attributes about you and think of three negative ones. Put the book down right now and literally do this.

Three Positive Attributes about Me:

1. ____

2. ____

3. ____

Three Negative Attributes about Me:

1. ____

2. ____

3. ____

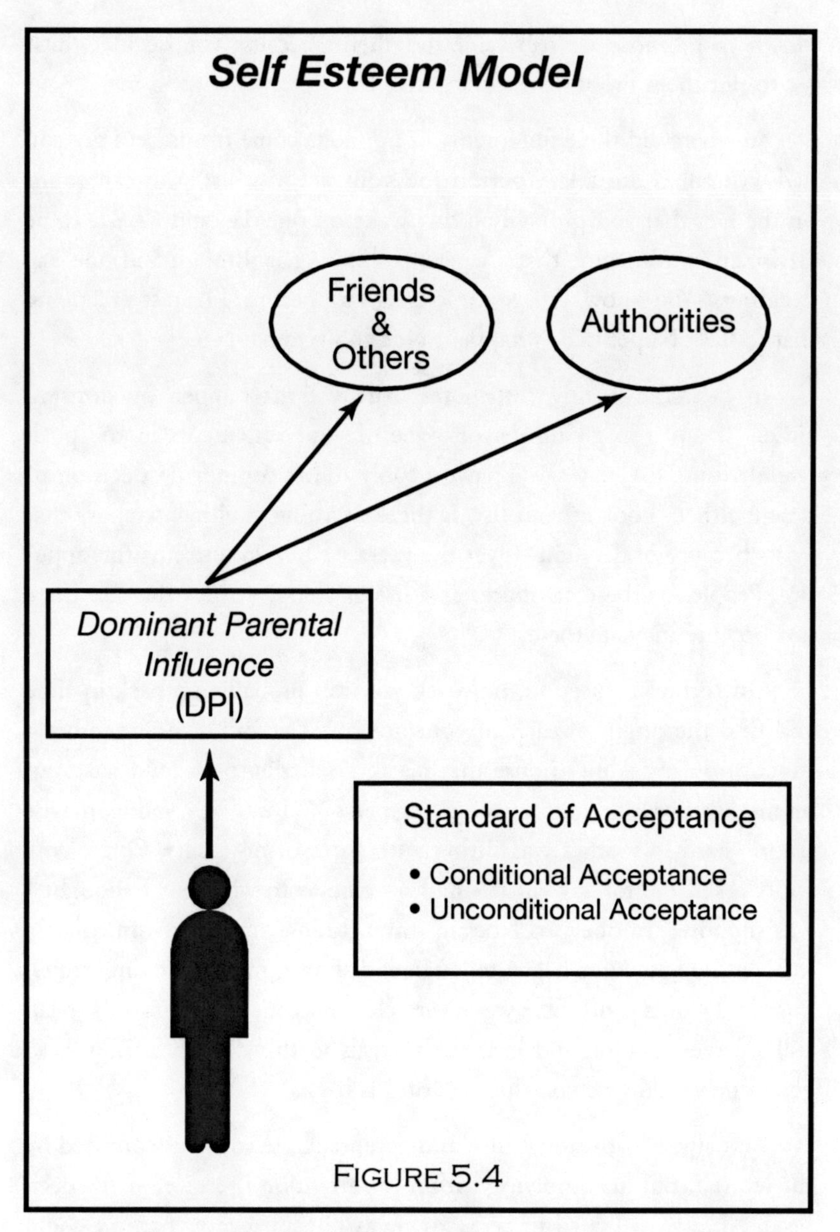

FIGURE 5.4

What did you think of? If you look at your list, you will notice a list of value judgments. You probably thought of attributes that have the same kind of tone or spirit as, "I am creative" as a positive attribute or something like, "I get angry too quickly" as a negative one. These are judgments about you, statements of value about who you are or how you are. Even if you gave descriptive phrases such as, "I am tall" or "I have brown hair," those are still value judgments because you decide which list to put them in, positive or negative.

So where did these judgments or opinions come from? Let's say you had written, "I am a lazy person" on your negative list. You can count on the fact that you probably didn't wake up one day and ***decide*** to be lazy. Can you imagine that? A person thinking it through and one day deciding, "You know, I'm going to be a lazy person. I'll start practicing that today!" Nope. Didn't happen. Not going to happen.

In fact, the positive attributes usually don't happen by decision either. "I am a forgiving person" one of your statements in the positive attribute list may say. That probably didn't come from decision or design either. Look at your list. Is there anything in either category that exists because of decision? Over the years we have found just the opposite. People see these attributes as a list of characteristics that are there just because they are there.

On further inspection, however, you can probably go back in time and find the origin of each of your attributes. I, Bill, can remember a situation in my Aunt's house that began an attribute I would have put on my positive list, "I am a very giving person." I was very young, maybe five or six. My mother was sitting with three of my aunts. One of my aunts asked me for my shirt. I had no clue as to why, but I thought I was supposed to obey, so I began unbuttoning my shirt. Immediately my Mother and aunts began to laugh and shower me with loving smiles, hugs and words. And there was a very clear message in their words. I can still see the situation and hear their words to this day, "See, Billy is so giving he would give you the shirt off his back."

Actually, I just wanted love and acceptance. And I was confused by the request. But in complying with it the attention I received met a deep need. After that, I tried to be as giving as possible every chance I could so as to get the same attention and acceptance. "I've grown out of this by now though, right Joann?"

Joann speaking: "He has grown out of the need for acceptance derived from a giving spirit, but he is still a very giving person. It is not always necessary to do so, but if you can trace a given attribute back to an early origin, you may find that something you do as a part of your normal nature was used to fulfill a certain need. Bill is still giving, but now his giving spirit flows freely, without hidden agenda, and not burdened with the baggage of need."

The point is, the lists you created aren't really positive or negative. They received their value judgment because of the situation or experience they were associated with. And this is how you came to "esteem" yourself. Under the dynamics of the model we are talking about, these attributes aren't really about you, they are about *how you think about you.* And each of these attributes was given to you by someone else. You didn't choose them; you are just living out your life's script. So, to be even clearer, what we are saying is this: ***Self esteem really isn't SELF esteem, it is DPI esteem.*** How your DPI esteemed you, amplified by the experiences of life, is how you came to view or esteem yourself. This is shown schematically in Figure 5.5

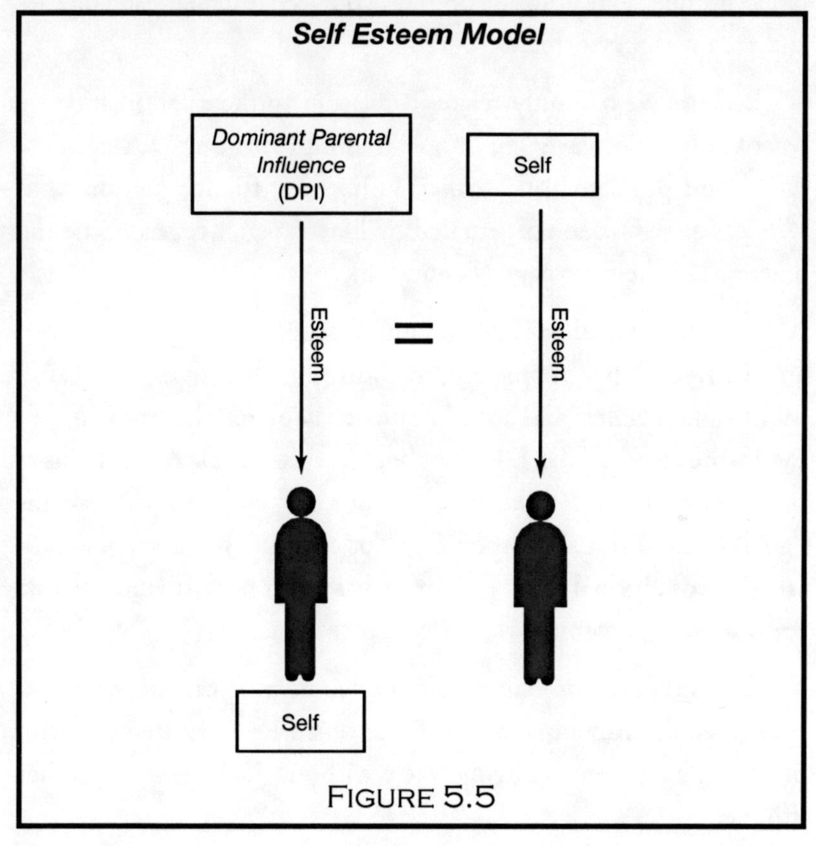

FIGURE 5.5

And this concept of a so called "self-esteem" that is based on our DPI perspective is perpetuated by our self-talk. You know, that inner voice, the one that gives comment about what and how you are doing. Try doing something a bit rebellious and notice what that inner voice says. What you will probably hear are comments similar to what your DPI would say. In fact, we have talked to some people who admit that their self-talk voice is, indeed, that of their DPI.

In regards to our self-esteem, we are walking through life living out the dynamics of our past. Here, again, the basic principles of programming are revealed. We are products of our past, making the best choices available to us, living out the same dynamics of previous experience and relationship.

If you experienced conditional acceptance from your DPI, that is what you give to yourself. You feel good about yourself or you feel bad based on how you did, not on who you are. Your self-esteem rises and falls with performance.

Because we can only relate in relation to the relationships we have known, our early childhood training with our DPI is transferred and projected onto other authorities, friends or others, as well as our self, then perpetuated by life's experience. Examine the diagram on the next page (Figure 5.6).

The diagram illustrates how most people are living life. They are not free. Other people are in control of their lives, (the DPI's list of values, beliefs and appropriate behavior, or whoever is standing in the stead of the DPI, i.e. boss, spouse, etc.). And, if this is the case, they have unhealthy or poor self esteems, self-esteems based on conditional acceptance. (Notice, if the standard of acceptance is conditional and "esteem" is based on performance, it isn't really a "self" esteem; it is "performance" esteem).

A healthy self esteem would be where you can be who you really are and truly possess a ***SELF*** esteem where *you* are in control of your life and *you* are living freely without the baggage of earlier experience.

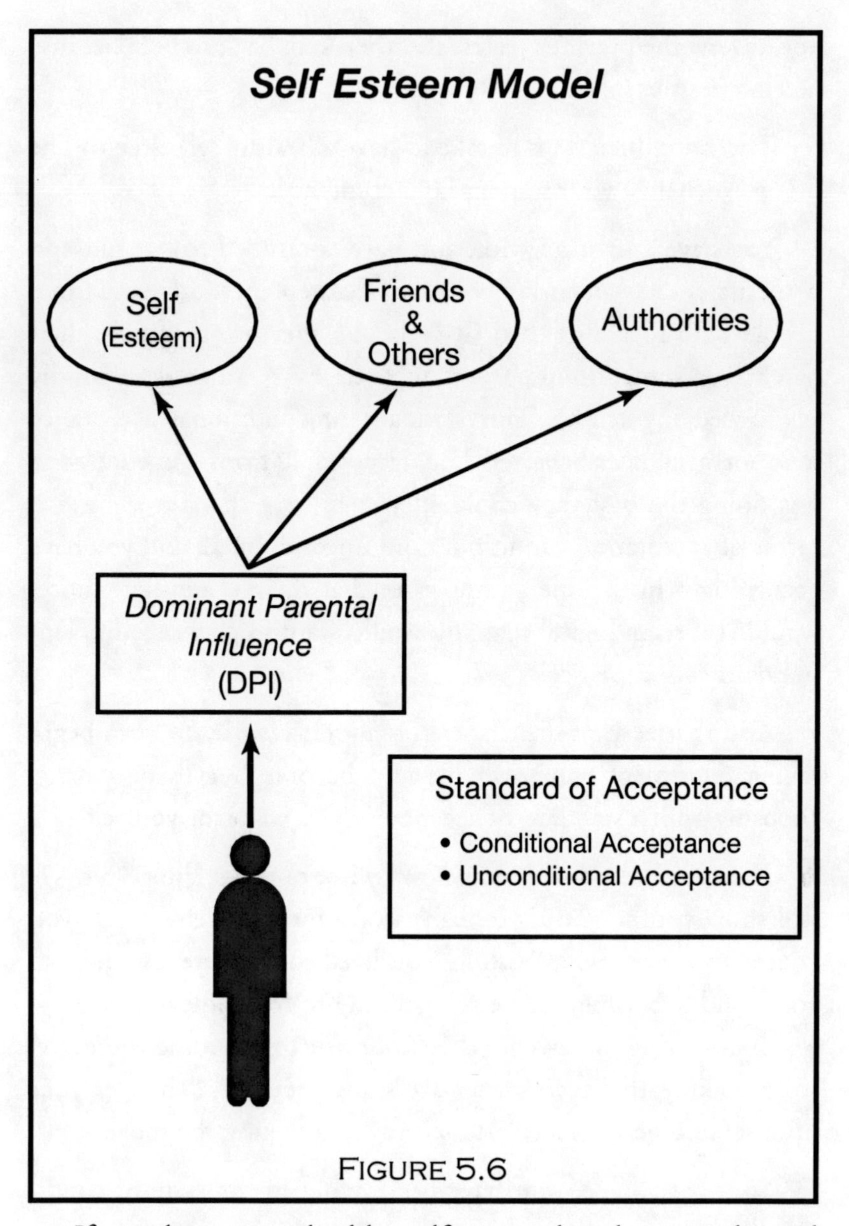

FIGURE 5.6

If you have an unhealthy self esteem based on conditional acceptance, and most likely you do since most of us fit into this dynamic, you are not trapped. There is freedom. It is important that you understand the problem clearly, however. We can then teach you how to have ***your own*** self esteem and live with unconditional acceptance. Do you understand the problem clearly? If not, review the previous pages, and then skip back to here because here comes the solution.

There are three steps to take to have a healthy self esteem. The first is to change your standard of acceptance.

You have grown up with, and have continued to live out and perpetuate, the standard of conditional acceptance. So many times people hate to admit this. (It feels like they are betraying their parents or someone important in their lives rather than simply acknowledging truth). This standard of conditional acceptance was not a choice, however. You received it from someone who was doing the best they could. If you can see that there are two forms of acceptance, conditional and unconditional, and you have been caught in the one and now see that there is another choice, wouldn't it seem logical that you would want to choose a different standard of acceptance?

And that is what the first step is about: ***choose.*** You can begin taking control of your own life and become free to be you by choosing which standard of acceptance you want for yourself.

Naturally, you don't know how to live out that choice yet. We will show you how. But you can't live somewhere else unless you choose to move there. Wishing you lived somewhere else, hoping you could live somewhere else, planning to live somewhere else—is still not living somewhere else. ***Choosing*** to live somewhere else, truly making the ***decision*** to live somewhere else, changes your mindset and gets the steps started toward making the move.

So, now you see you have been living in the state of conditional acceptance where your value and worth, your acceptance, is based on your behavior and performance. You also now see there is a new state to live in called unconditional acceptance where you have inherent value and worth simply because you are a human being. Your behavior flows from who you are and it is seen separately from your value as a person. Decisions about behavior come in the context of your behavior not your acceptance. The first perspective, the standard of conditional acceptance is unhealthy and limited; the second, the standard of unconditional acceptance, is healthy and free.

Which one do you choose for you?

Really—which one do ***you*** choose for ***you?*** You ***are*** free to choose. You don't have to perpetuate what has been given you.

We trust you choose unconditional acceptance as your standard of acceptance. But listen carefully to your choice. Some people have answered the question this way, "I ***want*** to choose unconditional acceptance," or "I will choose unconditional acceptance and see if I can stay with it or not."

Notice the problem with these perspectives. Wanting to choose is not choosing; it is simply wishing. And choosing to live out the unconditional standard of acceptance as long as you are able to do it is conditionally accepting unconditional acceptance. In other words, you are saying, "I choose it, but I will see if I have chosen it based on whether I can live it or not." You are basing your choice on performance or behavior which is nothing more than living out conditional acceptance. That's like deciding to quit smoking but basing your decision on whether you smoke or not.

So, don't wish or want, don't determine whether you have chosen by your behavior—***choose!***

Now, since you have chosen unconditional acceptance, note the time and date you did that because we have a marvelous concept to teach you right now.

Let's say you are reading this book on January 7 at 3:30 in the afternoon when you choose to live out the standard of unconditional acceptance. Here is the marvelous concept: At 3:30pm on January 7 you ***HAVE*** a healthy self esteem. How is that possible? Because, if conditional acceptance manifests itself, or results in, an unhealthy self esteem and unconditional acceptance creates a healthy self esteem and you have moved from one to the other by choice, you now have a healthy self esteem. It's logical—and real.

Of course, you don't know how to do it completely yet. But you are there, and living it is now a possibility. A parallel example would be if you decided to stop using the telephone and start using e-mail to connect with a friend. You have been spending an inordinate amount of money in long distance charges so you decide to stop using the phone and use the internet instead.

If you are not proficient with e-mail, if you are uncomfortable with e-mail, if you don't even have a computer to use e-mail yet—none of these issues changes your choice. But without your choice you will not, indeed, cannot, deal with these issues. And if you pick up the phone by habit or mistake, it still doesn't change your choice. You have simply and temporarily made a mistake. As soon as you see that, you revert back to your new choice. Your choice becomes the calibration point.

Good news, huh? You now ***have*** a healthy self-esteem. And it didn't take you years of therapy to get there. (We can hear the traditional therapists screaming about now). People who have spent hundreds and thousands of dollars in therapy have come to our Personal Growth Intensive and found the freedom that comes from this concept instantly. But, remember, this is just the first step. There are two more.

When you choose to have a healthy self esteem and let unconditional acceptance be your standard of acceptance, you now need to learn what that means and how to live it. Deciding to use e-mail for a person who is computer illiterate creates the need for a teacher, a coach, someone who can teach them how to do it.

When you reflect on the Self-Esteem Model you can notice that the most powerful component for teaching you conditional acceptance was your DPI. Logic follows that the highest leverage change in the model would be to choose a new DPI.

We're not talking about literally choosing a new parent but simply choosing someone else you can mentally slip into that box to learn from.

Ironically, no matter how poor or beaten down a person's self esteem, they can still *imagine* what it would be like to be unconditionally accepted. Further, they can find someone or something that can be a role model for that kind of acceptance.

We have had people choose a person they knew or know, a deceased person, a dog or a cat, a Divine entity, a make believe character, or any number of diverse beings. The goal here is not to choose a new parent but to choose a new role model.

What should happen as we grow up is this: Our craving for unconditional acceptance is met by an unconditionally accepting DPI—who teaches us how to accept our self. As we grow up, our DPI gradually lets go and enables us to be on our own in complete freedom and in control of our own life. We are then "parenting" our own self.

When we experience conditional acceptance we have the craving for unconditional acceptance we were born with met by conditionally accepting standards. We then go through life making others our DPI to try and have that need fulfilled so are constantly setting up or looking for that accepting parent.

What we're suggesting is like starting over. You are "reborn" with your choice to live out unconditional acceptance. You choose a DPI that can teach you what it means to be unconditionally accepted. You then live under that mentoring or teaching until you can parent yourself.

Specifically you do this: As you are living life, one of the habits that comes from your conditionally accepting past, is to beat yourself up for not doing your best, for making a major (or even minor) mistake. When you make a mistake or cause a problem, ask, "What would my new DPI say about this?" People always get this kind of answer, "You blew it, didn't you? You made an awful mistake. You are a valuable person. I accept you. Now what are you going to do about your mistake?"

This separates person from performance. And over time you learn to do this without asking your mental DPI. You learn to assess the problem, look carefully at the issues, and make a choice about what to do—all without letting your performance dictate your discouragement or lesson your value. Step two, then, is to learn from your chosen DPI what it is like to accept yourself, especially when your behavior is disappointing.

Step three is designed to keep you objective and remembering truth. The powerful concept and perspective "The truth shall set you free" is at the core of this third step. As long as you can maintain the truth of your choice and the truth of the dynamics within any given situation or moment, you can maintain your freedom—your freedom to be and your freedom to choose. When you lose sight of truth you are destined to repeat old patterns and default to old perspectives.

Step three is to treat everything as input or feedback. Your behavior, the words of others, evaluations, grades, how you feel about a certain task you performed—all are just bits of ***input** that determine how you did rather than who you are.* There is a simple tool and concept you can use to accomplish this step. Simply practice the phrase and believe the truth, "Everything is input."

If we looked you in the eye and said with power and conviction, "You are a tree," would that change your life? It would only if you accepted our words. Instead, your mind takes the words, evaluates them, determines that our words are not valid, then discards the content.

What if we were your trusted supervisors, people you looked up to and whose opinion you valued? What if you had a conditionally accepting mind set? And what if, given the previous two questions reality, we said, also with conviction and power, "You are a failure!"

There is no difference in the amount or weighting to our words, yet, if you accepted those words you become devastated. In fact, most people don't even evaluate the "input," they just swallow it and react accordingly. But, in reality, ***both*** statements are just input.

What you do, then, is to treat ***everything*** as input. Your behavior is probably from good intention. So you look at the effectiveness of your behavior and adjust accordingly until you get the outcome you desire. When someone else says something about you, first of all, that person has no right to control you or judge the value of your person. Their words then, even if couched in terms that are directed to you about your person, are really just input about how they perceived or received your behavior. It is input that you can make a choice about. If it is valid, you swallow it and deal with it by making appropriate choices. If it is not valid, (like you are a tree), you seek more information to determine the perspective of the person, and, when you understand their words (input) well, you make a decision about what you are going to do about that input.

Notice this, criticism ***or praise*** is still only input. Neither positive nor negative feedback makes you a better or worse person. It is simply input about your behavior or performance that needs to be accepted as just that—input. Then, if necessary, make decisions about that input.

You may be asking, "Isn't there some input that is about me as a person?" Even if a person says something like, "You are a good person," which doesn't seem to have any input about behavior, it is still coming from that person's perspective. And that person's value judgment about you being a "good person" is still being formed by the criteria in that person's mind or experience not on the truth that you are a valuable person regardless of what this person says. To believe you are a good person because of someone else's input sets up the logical conclusion that you can also be a bad person if another person speaks it so.

This concept is like looking at the speedometer in your car. If you are driving down the freeway and notice that your speedometer reads 35 MPH, you don't sit there in discouragement and believe you are always going to go 35 MPH. You don't wallow in the embarrassment that others are watching you go 35 MPH. Instead, you immediately make the decision to step on the accelerator and shoot your speed right up to ~~85~~ ~~75~~ 65. The speedometer only indicates the speed, it doesn't dictate it! It is input that motivates you to choose. It is feedback that is fuel for choice, it is not a decree that determines wherein you are stuck.

The underlying point is this: No one has the right or the ability to judge your worth and value as a person. You are inherently valuable because of your being. Actions or behavior are subject to opinion, judgment, like, dislike and a whole host of other reactions. They are separate from your person however and, though complex in perspective sometimes, are simply points of difference or discussion and are always subject to choice regarding how you, or anyone else for that matter, relate to them.

To reiterate, there are three steps to have and live out a healthy self esteem:

1. ***Choose the standard of unconditional acceptance as the way you will look at yourself and others.***
2. ***Choose a new "DPI role model" to show you what it is like to live with this standard.***
3. ***Treat everything as input, making decisions about what to do regarding that input but never letting the input determine your worth and value as a person.***

Now, watch yourself as you live out this new life with your healthy self-esteem. When you have unconditional acceptance as your standard of relating to yourself or others, you won't automatically reject anyone or belittle them for their mistakes. Everything is treated as an issue to deal with, a choice to make. If you find yourself sitting in discouragement about your performance, trying to look good for acceptance, or engaging with others in a non-objective way (getting sucked into arguments of worth or value—"you are a good-for-nothing so and so"), recognize that you have slipped back into an old habit. Revisit your choice, learn from what happened and move on in your freedom. To reflect on an earlier illustration, you have simply picked up the phone again (because it is a habit) and forgot, for the moment, that you have chosen to use e-mail.

So, can you lose a healthy self esteem? No, you can't—if you remember your choice. If your self-esteem is based on choice, not performance, you can't "lose" your self-esteem. You are free to choose conditional acceptance any time you want to. But you don't default to it just because you behave like it.

A wonderful aspect of having a healthy self-esteem is how it lets you treat others. You are no longer needy. You no longer look to others for acceptance. As a result, you can give yourself unconditional acceptance ***and*** give it to those around you – including your parents, even the one who was your DPI. This is a wonderful experience and makes for a great relationship.

Don lived life with such fear and wasted a lot of energy trying to live up to everyone else's expectations. He was burdened with the standard of conditional acceptance. He wasn't free and was always under a ton of stress. His health and relationships showed it. It seemed like nothing in Don's life was healthy.

He learned and began to practice the three simple steps in this chapter after he understood the perspective of the problem deeply. When he did, his life changed.

Actually, transformed would be a better word than "changed." Neither he nor anyone around him could believe the happiness, the freedom, and the confidence as well as the more meaningful effectiveness he enjoyed in relationships. Yet these were all the natural by-products of having a healthy self-esteem and living life with the standard of unconditional acceptance.

We trust you will practice this, too. When you do, you will have the same results. We know you can because we have seen it literally thousands of times. It is yours for the taking by simply exercising belief then choice. It really is that simple. And it really is that powerful.

What about the rest of the programming areas in our Basic Programming Model? What do we do with those? There are three ways to find your programs and three ways of re-programming the ones that are no longer effective. The next chapter will show you how to do just that. In fact, when you perform the steps in the next chapter you will have a complete understanding of what makes you tick and be able to predict your reaction and behavior in any situation.

Moreover, you will be in complete control of your self, living life on purpose!

How does it feel to grow up and begin taking control of your own life and parenting yourself? Scary? That's normal. Allow yourself to feel that. We will address how to cleanse from the feelings of fear and loss in chapter 8. Hang in there. It will be ok. Though you have made a decision, there is a process to go through to realize the benefits of your decision.

In fact, with decision there comes process. That is normal and necessary. When you decide to plant a garden, that decision directs you and is the powerful step that makes you a gardener. After that decision and the truth therein, there is a process you go through until you are able to reap a bountiful harvest from that garden.

We know these dynamics well. One time, long ago, we were hungry too. We made decisions. Now we are able to feast on abundance in happiness and freedom, in confidence and personal power, in peace and fulfillment. You too? Yes, most decidedly, you too!

Patience.

Chapter 6

Finding Your Programs

...Understand how your programs are manifested in your life

Patty seemed to be a bit controlling. Yet, by her own admission, she didn't *seem* to be controlling; she was controlling. Not all the time, just when a friend wanted to do something with her, just when her husband had a different opinion or idea, just when she was delegating work to her staff, just when…well, you get the idea. She said she couldn't help herself, and, until she attended the PGI, she couldn't.

What was going on with Patty? It was a simple case of living out her past dynamics and programs, one major one in particular. Patty felt the full weight of ensuring her family's happiness and well being as she was growing up. In fact, as she described the program she was following, she found she portrayed herself as Atlas holding up the world. "It felt that heavy," she said.

You understand the principles that cause this to happen by now. Suffice it to say, at a very early age, Patty learned that she was responsible to make everyone in her family happy and healthy. The dynamics of her program also taught her that if she didn't take care of those around her, her very happiness and survival were at stake. So she had to do what she thought was best for everyone else and ***make sure*** that it happened every time or else she and the family member she was taking care of at the moment were in jeopardy. No one could alter from her desire, plan or perspective. It was too dangerous. She had to be in control. And her family let her.

So every time she was in a position to take care of someone, be responsible for someone, share her perspective or opinion, or simply decide with a friend where to have lunch—her program would fire and she had to be the one to be in control. Her subconscious mind told her it was too dangerous to do otherwise.

From today's perspective her behavior and attitude look simply predictable. Earlier, when she was draped in the heavy mantel of responsibility from her insistent and insidious program, she was confused, unhappy and constantly stressed. Her health and her relationships suffered.

Now Patty understands her program and is in control of it. She is free and happy. And others around her are pleased about that, too—it makes their life easier.

How did Patty find her program and change it? She used a combination of the three methods we're going to teach you in this chapter to find her program; then she changed it with the tools in the next chapter. When you give attention to these three indicators, you can understand what your programs are in every aspect of our basic programming model.

Remember this, however: different aspects of the model have different levels of power or influence over us. Driver programs are embedded deeply in our subconscious. They greatly influence our attitude, behavior and perspective. They are usually more prevalent but somewhat harder to change and sometimes hard to own. Sometimes people are reluctant to acknowledge that their programs exist. They don't want to face themselves because they are too embarrassed, too afraid, or just plain too dissatisfied with what they see.

Driver programs may never leave us, but we can be in full control of them. Both of us have deeply rooted driver programs that fire frequently…as do you. Some time ago there would be a rather large gap of time between when the program fired and when we were able to be in control of the program. It used to be that the program would fire, we would automatically succumb to it, wallow in its weirdness for awhile, suffer the effects from it, then, eventually, understand what was going on and use the remedies we will teach you later in the next chapter.

Now it is a matter of seconds (or less) between the time a program fires and when we are in control of it. In fact, many of our programs are gone, others just give out weak whimpers now and then, and still others, especially the driver programs, fire frequently but have no power. And that is freedom. Anytime we allow anyone or anything, even a program, be in control of us, we are not free. When we are able to make choices about life, we are free. We will show you how to manage and control your programs in the next chapter. Just know that your driver programs will have a long shelf life.

The other programs in the model have differing levels of power denoted by their names: Filters, Attracters, and Influencers. Figure 6.1 below is a reiteration of the model for your review.

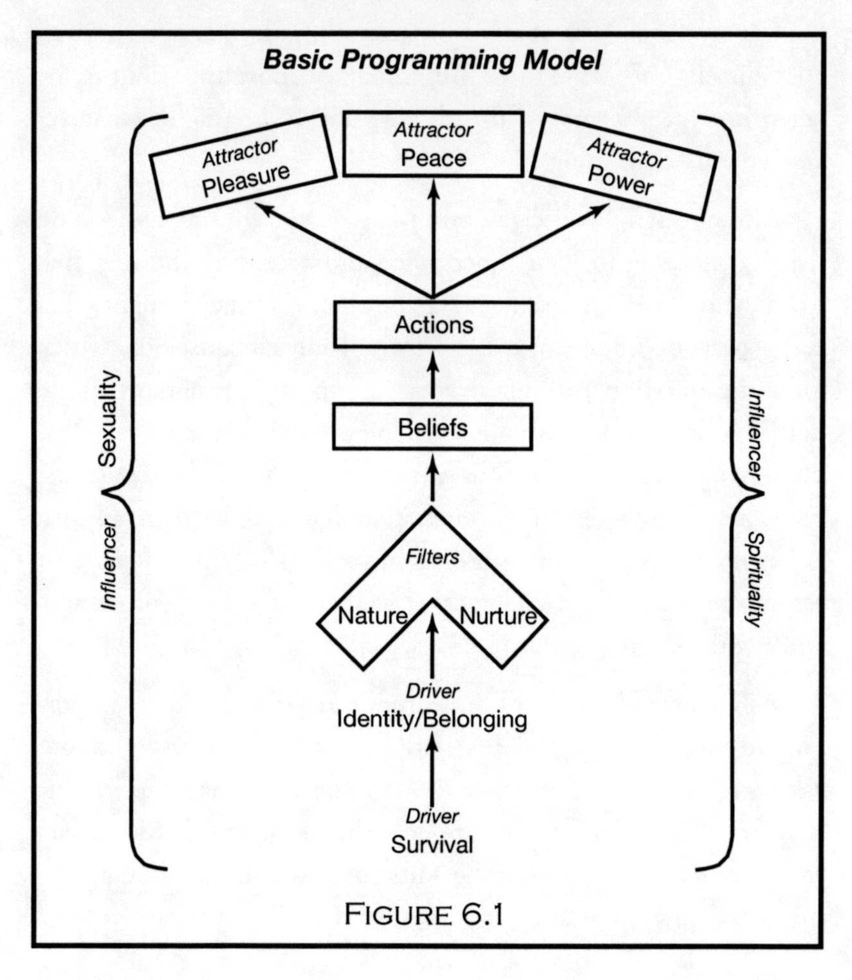

FIGURE 6.1

There are three ways to decipher your programs. These three ways are:

1. Questioning for analysis

2. Finding repetitive attitudes or behaviors

3. Observing incongruent emotions or reactions

The first method you can use to find your programs is to ask simple, yet specific questions about the programming area you are analyzing. It is an overt way to analyze your programs. I, Bill, will illustrate this process in the context of my survival programs. First, an explanation of the method.

For any one of the areas of programming, in this case survival, ask yourself, "What are three things that are most important to me when it comes to survival (or identity and belonging or whatever area you are examining)?"

Allow your subconscious mind to give you the answer. You do that by listening to your inner voice and accepting the very first words you "hear" yourself saying. Beware, the first thoughts that come to your mind are usually from your subconscious, which links the question to your deeper responses or programs. In so doing, your response may not seem logical, so you change it. What often happens is our conscious mind notices the subconscious first response, doesn't like it or doesn't understand it, then adjusts, edits or changes the response all together. Listen to your first response no matter how illogical it seems. We'll show you how to work with that response to make sense of it.

Ask yourself for a list of three important things that are important to you. Though there is nothing sacred or necessary about asking for a list of three, there seems to be some magic to it. One item may not be sufficient to get a theme or trend. More than three seems to get too cumbersome or redundant. Though you may not come up with three things, start with that parameter and notice what answer come. Write down any number of responses that come to you.

When I, Bill, asked myself the question, the three things that came to me were:

1. Food
2. A person
3. A horse

Notice how illogical these answers are. You will see how they make sense in a bit. For now, notice something that is consistent with everyone who does this exercise. The "logical" answers of food, clothing, and shelter, often don't exist in their entirety in most people's answers. The reason is this: Your answers are coming from your survival programs that are experience-based, not from the logical perspective of what is necessary for a human being to survive. Whatever you *learned* is important to you.

We have mentioned some people already in this book who have had very individual perspectives on what is important for them to survive. Remember the man who needed to keep a number of people together to make a "herd" for survival? We also worked with a woman who needed light, a man who needed orientation, a woman who needed knowledge, a man who needed a weapon—all different, all important to each person, no item necessarily important to another person.

I remember one woman who had to have shelter. That isn't important to me at all. Though I probably would want shelter and quite probably obtain it at some point, my deepest survival programs do not include shelter. And, as you will recall earlier in the book, whenever a survival dynamic occurs, my survival programs will fire and I will want food, a person and a horse—not light, not clothes, not shelter, not orientation, not a weapon—just food, a person and a horse. But what does that mean?

Our "illogical" first responses are only illogical to our conscious minds, just as these were to mine, but they make sense to our subconscious mind. What we need to do is follow the trail backward to determine what the subconscious is thinking about. To do that, you ask a follow-up question to the first one.

After you have asked yourself what the three things are that are most important to you for survival, you then ask, "What do I get out of that?" for each of the responses. You keep asking that question until there are no more answers.

For example, for the item on my list, "a person," I asked the question, "What do I get out of that?" and the answer was companionship. I then asked about companionship, "What do I get out of that?" and the answer was help, support, strength. When I asked, "What do I get out of *that?"* no other answer came.

Notice, the first response was a clue or a link to the more specific core response. I really didn't want a person as much as I was wanting additional support and strength. And remember, we are asking the question in this case in the context of survival. If the answers about needing a person seemed to be about companionship, love, relationship, etc, it would indicate that I was really focused on the other driver program of identity and belonging, not survival.

In fact, we have seen many people do just that. They default to relationship needs when they begin looking for survival programs because of the power in the identity and belonging program. That's why we chose to deal with your self-esteem or your identity and survival programs first, in the last chapter, before addressing other areas of programming.

One of the reasons your identity and belonging program seems to ride piggyback on the answers you receive for other programming areas is this: Most people have their survival needs met. The most powerful driver program they are experiencing, then, is the need for identity and belonging. When they ask themselves the questions about what is most important to them regarding any other area in our programming model, the powerful programs surrounding identity and belonging tend to seep into all of the answers. When you begin doing your questioning and searching for your programs, whether you are asking the question regarding pleasure, peace, power, spirituality sexuality or one of the filters, be careful to not let your driver programs infiltrate. Stay focused on the particular area you are asking about.

To restate, the process is to ask, "What are three things that are most important to me when it comes to survival?" Then you follow-up with each of your responses with the question, "What do I get out of that?" until you have found the core answer or program.

You will notice, then, that whenever you encounter your program's dynamics, that program will fire and you will automatically do what you have always done unless you reprogram or manage yourself and your program. For me, when it looks like I will be alone, my survival program fires. I feel fear. I may lose focus on other issues. And I am driven to satisfy the program's dictate to find someone to support me—that is, I used to be that way until I learned how to reprogram and/or manage my programs, something you will learn later in the next chapter.

My other answers about what is important to me regarding survival, food and a horse also had trails that lead back to the core issue. The core need that surrounded the answer, "a horse," had to do with mobility. In tracing back to the answer, I found that freedom of movement and something that enabled me to move more quickly than on my own accord was extremely important to me. A horse, a bicycle, a car—all could satisfy this need or program.

This program of mobility to survive, along with my need for the support of a person, came from the learning I received as a child from my father. He was a cowboy and taught me cowboy ethics, one of which is the need for a partner to survive in this life, another is the need to have the ability to move freely to a place that has what you need to survive. Though in some ways these concepts seem unnecessary or illogical, and though they were not consciously taught to me by my father, nevertheless, my young mind captured these concepts and they became very real survival programs for me.

The real need surrounding the surface need for food came partly from physiology and partly from learning. I have a high metabolism and a nervous system that needs fuel. If I don't get enough food, I don't sleep well, I get light headed, and I don't have sufficient strength. The learned aspect of my program came from my mother whom I talked about in Chapter Four. You will recall that she needed an abundance of food because of her young days of insufficiency. So part of my food survival program is legitimately necessary and working for me; another part isn't.

And this is what you do with the information from this questioning search. You ask yourself, "Is this working for me? Is it limiting me in anyway? Am I free to have other responses?" If your program is not working for you by causing you some kind of dysfunction or pain or fear, if your program is limiting you in any way and takes away any degree of freedom, then you need to change it with the managing and reprogramming techniques in the next chapter. If your programs are not debilitating in any way, you can leave them the way they are.

I had to change a few of my survival programs to keep from being dysfunctional. When I did, it became okay to be alone. It was okay not to have leftovers at a meal. I no longer felt trapped if I didn't have some form of transportation. My programs no longer had the power to limit my freedom or limit my choices. For each of the areas on our programming model you can walk through this process to find your programs.

You already know about the standard programs that fire for everyone in the area of identity and belonging, but you can still ask the question there, too. You may find that the underlying issues that surround acceptance may be manifesting themselves in some specific way. For example, you may find that you always shrink in the presence of certain types of people, educated professionals, for instance. Or you may find that you automatically reject certain types of people, men for instance, or women, or maybe certain cultures or age groups of people. The exploration in the area of identity and belonging can help you see how your acceptance program is specifically being played out.

You can even do the questioning analysis for the filter areas of nature and nurture. These areas can be daunting, however, since there is so much in our past experience (nurture) and our genetic expressions (nature). To make the questioning manageable and helpful in the two filter areas, we suggest you focus on only a few high-leverage areas to see if you have any limiting or dysfunctional programs firing.

In the nature area, focus on your gender and your culture. Regarding your gender ask, "What are the three most important things to me when it comes to being a man or a woman?" When you look at your culture you will first need to determine what "culture" means to you. It may be your cultural heritage (French), it may be your geographic culture (American, even though you are French), or it may be more of an informal and focused culture such as farmer, cowboy, New Englander, etc. Once you determine what your focal point is regarding culture, you can ask the exploration question, "What are the three most important things to me when it comes to being a Frenchman/American/farmer/New Englander, etc?"

With "nurture," the highest leverage places to look for programs are in the areas of love and fear. Remember the first time you experienced love. (And, notice, we're saying ***experienced*** love, not when you knew you were loved). Notice the dynamics that surround that experience. What messages and meanings surround it? What was acceptable or not acceptable? What did you learn at that moment? The answers to those questions will give you clues as to your programs that surround the experience of feeling love. Do the same thing with the first time you experienced fear. These two situations create programs in the nurture component that you carry through life – unless you consciously choose to change what is not working well for you.

The focus is easier in the other areas of the programming model: Pleasure, Peace, Power, Spirituality, and Sexuality. Ask the exploration question; follow it up with the question, "What do I get out of that?" and you will have a great understanding of the basic programs that govern your attitude and behavior.

Stop now and do the following exercise so you can begin finding your programs.

1. Ask yourself, "What are the three things that are most important to me when it comes to…"

- ***Survival***
- ***Identity and Belonging***
- ***Nature (Gender, Culture)***
- ***Nurture (Feeling love, Feeling fear)***
- ***Pleasure***
- ***Peace***
- ***Power***
- ***Spirituality***
- ***Sexuality***

2. After you have the answers, ask "What do I get out of that?" for anything that seems illogical.

As mentioned, there are two more ways to find your programs. The questioning way we have described is designed to help you do an overt search. The next two ways are used after a program has already fired. These two tools will help you follow the trail back to the origin of your programs, programs you may have been previously unaware of.

Have you ever found yourself repeatedly having the same response to the same kind of experience? You find yourself having the same attitude and behavior every time a certain situation happens? This would be a clue that a program is firing. The specific tool we are talking about is to notice repetitive attitudes and behaviors that surround situations with similar dynamics.

I, Joann, will illustrate this one. I know that I am a very giving person. Sometimes Bill says I may give too much. Just the other night, in our son's restaurant, I persuaded Bill to give a much larger tip to the server than we usually do simply because I felt it was important. I didn't have any logic to support it, I just felt it. And Bill supported my wish.

Many times I have been willing to give to others, give of myself and of our resources—except when my subconscious senses that I am being taken advantage of. One of my programs is the fear of being out of control, which is deeply rooted as a survival program. This program can be manifested when a person is taking advantage of me (they are then in control, not me). Any time I perceive that someone is taking advantage of me, my program fires and I become fearful, angry, and protective and not as giving. I turn 180 degrees away from my natural self to be just the opposite when my program fires. Normally I would be willing to abundantly give to you if you were in need—but when my program is firing, don't you dare take a dime.

Over time I found that this reaction occurred consistently, though not often. I was confused at first because the situations where I felt this need to protect and withhold seemed so different: a friend kept something they borrowed longer than I expected, a person not giving as much of their time and energy to a project or task that I was pouring my heart into, someone not thanking me when I gave something to them.

Even as I write about this, it seems so petty, childish and completely unlike me. I would even feel a bit embarrassed after my reactions. Confused about it all, I finally understood when I looked at the ***underlying dynamics*** of the situations that caused the response, not the situations themselves. When I did, the puzzle was solved. I found that each of the situations had the same dynamics, that of someone else doing something that I couldn't control within the context of seemingly taking something away from me, i.e. the loaned item, equity of contribution to a task or project and deserved thanks.

Remember, the programs and the reactions aren't logical; they are just there. The goal is to identify them, understand them, and then be in control of the program rather than allowing the program to be in control of us. My program, though illogical and unnecessary in my present world, my program, though embarrassing and counterproductive, my program was—my program. I didn't choose it, but I learned it, and it was having an effect in my life until I mastered it.

This is an illustration of what may be happening in your life. We're suggesting that you simply become aware of your attitude and behavior responses and watch for consistencies. Look for types of people, situations or circumstances that seem to consistently cause you to feel and act in a certain way. This will be a clear clue that a program has fired.

Do the following exercise now to find potential programs.

1. Identify situations where you have a consistent response that is negative or unwanted.
2. Identify the <u>dynamics</u> of the situation. (How would you describe the situation in objective descriptive terms? What are the roles in the situation, i.e. authority figure, subordinate, etc? How do they interact?)
3. What past dynamic parallels the situation you are describing? (Look for situations with similar roles and interactions).

We will show you how to reprogram or manage the programs you find. For now, simply focus on how to find your programs. And now we will look at the third way to find your programs. This one, also, is designed to find a program after it has fired.

The third way to find your programs has to do with looking for incongruent emotional responses. These responses will undoubtedly result in behavior, but we are focused primarily on your emotional response.

By "incongruent" we mean you are experiencing a level or intensity of emotion that, from a more distant or logical perspective, doesn't match the level or intensity of the experience. Let's say something legitimately causes you anger. On an arbitrary anger intensity scale of 1 to 10, a normal reaction might be a 2 from an objective and reasonable perspective. But you find yourself exhibiting an intensity of 8 or 9. This would be an incongruent response. The intensity of the anger is incongruent with the intensity of the experience. When you observe these kinds of incongruent responses you can be virtually certain a program has fired.

The incongruent emotion can be *any* incongruent emotion, (too much affection, too much laughter, too much sadness, too much jealousy) but typically we see the incongruence manifested by an increased amount of fear, anger or insecurity toward a situation that doesn't merit it. These types of feelings are prevalent when a program is firing.

Do the following exercise now to find potential programs.

1. Identify situations where manifested incongruent emotions.
2. Identify the dynamics of the situation. (How would you describe the situation in objective descriptive terms? What are the roles in the situation, i.e. authority figure, subordinate, etc? How do they interact?)
3. What past dynamic parallels the situation you are describing? (Look for situations with similar roles and interactions).

The reason these feelings are associated with a program that is firing is because of the reason a program fires in the first place. A program fires when one or more of the nine areas in the programming model is threatened. If survival is threatened, our survival program fires; if identity is threatened; our identity program fires; if pleasure is threatened; our pleasure program fires—and so on. Associated with threat are the feelings of fear or anger or insecurity. It follows, therefore, that these feelings are indicators that a program is firing.

An example of this would be my, Bill's, survival program of being alone. In the past, something as simple as being home alone while my wife was gone with the car could fire my survival program of needing mobility. I would feel fear, incongruent fear. There was no need for the fear at all. The fear was associated with, and an indicator of, the unnecessary, but real, survival program that was firing.

In the next chapter we'll show you what to do once you've found your programs. For now go hunting to find your programs and how they are manifested in your life. Consciously do the questioning to analyze the nine areas in the programming model. Take an observer's stance and look at your life to find repetitive reactions and situations where your emotional response was incongruent to the experience. When you do this, you will not only have the understanding from the previous chapters of this book on what makes you tick, but you will also understand ***how*** you tick, how these programs affect you, your life and your relationships with others.

What's that we hear in you? Fear? Apprehension? Hesitancy? Naturally, you'd feel that; you're normal.

Jack feels that fear. At the time of this writing, we are talking to him about coming to a Personal Growth Intensive. He is 56 years old. He has been in the military, fought in many battles during the Viet Nam war, and has been in law enforcement. With managed fear that others would call fearless, he has faced the enemy many times and is still alive. Sometimes he wonders how and why. He is a strong and seasoned man. He is a gun dealer, a protector of the weak, and a role model for those who would be strong.

But amidst this life of grit and seemingly endless victories over enemies he could see, Jack has constantly battled the enemies he cannot see. They are enemies deep inside him. He knows they are there; he can feel them.

These enemies are his programs that constantly fire causing him no end of fear, frustration and pain. They have caused him to seek solution in alcohol, but that only gave him the identity of alcoholic. He tried to find fulfillment in marriage, but after four wives he has all but given up on having another relationship, believing his enemies within will continue to prevent and sabotage any attempt at intimacy.

So Jack copes. He has learned to cope all his life. His programs provide a way to cope, to get through life. Unfulfilled, unhappy and lonely, he has learned how to survive.

But even he admits, it's no way to live, really live. He is at a point where his thick and protective coping programs that have shrouded him for so long have worn enough to let life's longings through. And his once bullet-proof vest now has holes where shells of reality have made it through to pierce his heart with loneliness and unhappiness.

So we talk. We talk about hope and help. We talk about the thousands of people who have been helped by the principles in this book taught in the Personal Growth Intensive. And his fear grows. So much that we are uncertain as to whether he will take the steps to learn what you are learning.

He has faced many enemies but is afraid to face himself. To some extent, this is normal. Nearly everyone who goes through the process to this point has felt the fear that comes with facing reality. You may be feeling it right now. It's ok. Go through the fear. Don't be afraid of it.

If things get overwhelming, seek help from a therapist or a good friend. You are not "sentenced to life" with your life. Whatever you find that is not working, that is dysfunctional, or that is simply something that you want to change—***you CAN do it!***

And, right now, don't worry about fixing what you find; just identify and own what you find. Give yourself the unconditional acceptance you have already learned about. Every program, no matter how ugly or embarrassing, no matter how simple or complex, is just that—a program. They are simply puppet strings you did not choose. But you can choose to cut them and give yourself your own freedom. We will show you how.

So put on the armor of objective perspective and pick up the sword of truth. Let your heart beat with the courage of love, acceptance and understanding. Be strong in the support of thousands of others who have gone before you. Slay the dragon of fear who breathes the destructive fires of doubt. Let the light of truth illuminate your reality and give you the gift of understanding. Then bring that understanding into the next chapter and let us lead you to greater freedom, filled with productive days and peace-filled nights.

Chapter 7

Managing, Changing and Eradicating Your Programs

...Getting Ultimate Control of Your Own Life

We bought a new car and were pleased with it. It was probably the best car we had ever owned. But one day something went wrong. The temperature gage was fluctuating and the "check engine" light came on.

From an outside perspective nothing seemed wrong. The car ran fine, looked fine, sounded fine, smelled fine—only the instruments were telling us that something wasn't right.

We became cautious. Our drive wasn't going very well. It was continuously interrupted. We kept stopping to see if something was wrong. Slowly we made our way home then called a mechanic. The next day he checked the car with his computerized analysis system. Simply plugging this tool into the car's connection device told him the truth.

It appeared as though everything in the engine pertaining to the smog system had gone wrong. Every reading was showing a problem. But the analysis device continued to read and finally told the truth—it wasn't something that was really wrong, it was that some of the preinstalled programs had misfired.

Interesting parallel, wouldn't you say? Here you are, born into this world, an incredible human being, ready, receptive, valuable and filled with potential. Then programs are installed. Not programs you choose, installed still the same. Powerful programs that take over the guidance system of your being and pre-determine your performance and perspective.

One day you become aware that "the drive isn't going so well." On the outside things look fine, but on the inside there are gauges that are indicating, "Something isn't right." You tend to overheat. Your "check innards" light has come on.

So you picked up this book—the analysis tool—and you find that some of the pre-installed programs are misfiring. And that has caused your drive to be interrupted. You haven't been able to go as fast or as far as you wanted. Instead, you have had to keep stopping to see if everything is ok.

Can you relate? Did you use the tools in the last chapter to find the programs that are misfiring? Did you find, for example, that your acceptance program was putting out a false reading, telling you that you had to live up to everyone's expectations to be accepted? Did you find a survival or sexual or spiritual or power program that served you a long time ago, but is now no longer needed, yet you have perpetuated it because of habit?

The work of the last chapter was to help you find your programs. That work, along with all the understandings in the previous chapters, is the analysis tool that helps you see the truth about you—who you are, why you are the way you are, and why you do the things you do. The analysis tool has revealed how the rainbow you see has been created, how and where it shines, how bright it shines as well as why it is the way it is. You have seen the truth.

Truth. Sometimes hard to see, other times hard to accept, always the entrée to living more freely and more fulfilled.

In fact, without the truth of what is, you cannot change anything. Awareness and ownership about the truth are two parts of the first step in any growth or change. After that comes choice about what you want to do then the specific learning of what to do. Following that is the implementation and practice of your chosen direction, getting feedback along the way for continued course correction towards ultimate success.

So do you choose now to do something about the programs that have been hindering your progress, programs that keep you from being free? We know you do since you have read this far.

This chapter will teach you the three ways to be in control of your programs and prevent them from being in control of you. All three involve perspective and choice, seeing clearly what is going on then making a choice about what you want—living life on purpose. The three methods are:

1. Acknowledge the truth about a program
2. Change the structure of a program to reduce its power
3. Reprogram an unwanted behavior, attitude or response

Each of the three methods has a unique approach and application. The first one is the easiest to use and the gentlest in its power. The first method can be used for many of the less powerful programs. It can also be used for stronger programs that have weakened by your using the second or third methods listed above.

The second method takes a bit more effort and can be used for programs that have a comparatively stronger power than programs you would use method one for. Method two changes the outcome of a program by changing the sequence with which it fires, thus reducing its power.

The third method takes more time and effort still, yet it is designed to reprogram the subconscious firing of a program to dramatically reduce its power—many times to the point of elimination.

All three methods presuppose that you understand the principles in the book so far including what the program is and why it is firing, that is, what need it is serving or what programming area it is fulfilling. Embedded in this understanding is the concept of acceptance. You accept yourself; you understand and accept your programs. and you are willing to address them, to take control of your own life.

There is another powerful concept embedded in what we have just said. If you know yourself, including your programs, and you are willing to deal with those programs, and you are planning to use the concepts in this chapter to manage and reprogram your dysfunctional programs—all of that indicates that you are living your life by choice. You are, in essence, living life freely (though you may not be free from all of your past baggage, which we will show you how to do in the next chapter). You are not going to be a product or a victim of your past. You are going to take hold of your future and re-design it to be what you want it to be, not what the inertia of your life has previously dictated it to be.

It's an inalienable right and a wonderful feeling to live your life based on choice, to not have anything or anyone else in control of you. We believe that *living life freely, on purpose, with purpose* is the ultimate way to live.

So continue to take control of your life and exercise your choice as you learn how to use these three methods for managing and reprogramming your self.

The first method, "Acknowledging the truth about the program," is rather simple but powerful. It can change your response instantly. We'll tell you how it works.

The key component here is that you know your program and its response. For example, take my, Bill's, survival program of not wanting to be alone. If that program fires (and I knows it is firing because I recognize how it feels and what my response is) the first method simply says I need to acknowledge the truth about what is going on. "I'm facing dynamics that would suggest that I am going to be alone. I'm feeling fearful because the survival program I found believes that I will die if I am alone. Truth is, I am probably not going to be alone, and even if I am, I am not going to die. My program is a dysfunctional one that is no longer applicable in my life."

Now, this is a lengthy iteration of the truth, but it illustrates the core content of what can be done to demolish a program.

Here is another example: Authority figures, especially critical or judging ones, would tend to make me nervous due to my acceptance/rejection identity program. A simple, yet truthful statement dramatically helped when I was learning to manage that program. The statement was this, "This is not my mom!"

That statement had many truths associated with it. If it is not my mom, I can look at what is really going on and be more objective. The statement also reminds me of my chosen standard of acceptance, that of unconditional acceptance. I'm reminded that my behavior does not determine who I am, and the authority I am dealing with is simply that—an authority, someone I respect and will listen to, but not someone who determines my worth, value, or acceptance.

The first method, therefore, builds on what you found in the previous chapter. You know your programs; you understand the truth about them and you choose to live in that present truth rather than in past dynamics. When you do this, you are experiencing the basic principle *"The Truth shall set you free."*

The second method is about restructuring your program. Let's talk about the concept of how a program works first.

As with any computer program or a program that governs the thermostat in your home, there are a series of events that occur. Those events are sequential, one leading to the other until there is an outcome. If you change any aspect of the programmed sequence, you change the outcome.

Look at the simple program system for the heat in your home. Let's say the thermostat is set to turn on your heater when the temperature drops below 72 degrees. Everything is at rest until the sun goes down causing the room temperature to drop to 70 degrees. When that happens the program fires and looks something like this: Room temperature gets cooler, the metal spring in the thermostat gets smaller, two contact points connect, electricity flows to the heater to turn it on, the fuel is released into the burn chamber, the pilot light ignites the fuel, the sensor in the heater turns on the blower, and, finally, warm air blows into the room to warm it up.

Now, everything stays the same until the room temperature climbs above 72 degrees. Then: Room temperature gets warmer, thermostat spring expands, contact points disconnect...etc. The "cool down" program fires reversing the previous program's outcome. If you change the thermostat's temperature setting, the program changes. In fact, you can change *any* aspect of this sequence of events and the outcome would change—putting a cooling fan on the thermostat, using a harder spring so it would expand and contract differently, corrosion on the contact points, turning off the electricity to the circuit, and so on.

It's the same with our programs. In fact, there is an interesting study within the science of Neuro-Linguistic Programming that shows how it works. The studies are beyond the scope of this book but a mention will shed some light on your programs.

At its simplest form, a program's sequence involves the three senses you use most: sight, sound and touch or feeling (visual, auditory and kinesthetic). Every program that fires in you has content that is within these three elements. So you may see something, then feel something, then "hear" something (talk to yourself in your head, or hear self-talk, or literally hear something), then see something else, then hear something else, then feel something—all sequencing into a program. There can be multiple components of "visual, auditory, kinesthetic" in any order. The elements, the amount of elements and the order are determined by the first experiences that "programmed" you.

The concept above holds true. If you change any aspect of the sequenced elements you change the outcome. If seeing a highway patrolman causes you to feel anxious because it reminds you of your DPI, which then causes you to shake and stammer, which causes you to be defensive with the patrolman, which causes you to become fearful and therefore lash out in anger—that is a predictable program.

Method one tells us to speak the truth the moment the program fires, that is, the moment you feel nervous in the presence of a patrolman or authority figure. Method two goes beyond that.

Let's say you have tried to use method one, but the program is strong enough that you can't change it. Or, every time the program fires, you get sucked into the stream so quickly that you are not even aware of what is happening until after the program has run its course. If this is the case, use method two which is about changing the structure of a program.

We will teach you a visualization exercise that is designed to interrupt your program's sequence at a subconscious level. At this deeper level, you are interacting with the various components of visual, auditory and kinesthetic input from the experience. Every bit of input becomes a conditioned response that dictates your actions, the red or blue light on the patrolman's car, his uniform, the sound of his words, how your body feels, etc. The following exercise changes all of this, thus changing the sequence of the experience or program and fulfilling the criteria for method two's success—change the structure of the program and you change the outcome.

The visualization exercise starts by imagining an empty movie theater. There are going to be three parts of you in this exercise. First, on the screen, there will be a movie showing you getting a ticket from the highway patrolman. But that is not where you will be watching the scene from.

Imagine another part of you sitting in the middle of the theater preparing to watch the movie. That "you" may be eating popcorn, drinking a soda, sitting patiently while waiting for the movie to begin. But there is still another "you" in this exercise.

Imagine another "you" walking up to the projection booth and looking out the window into the theater. This is the perspective you will take as you do this exercise. You are in the projection booth, watching the "you" in the theater watch "you" on the screen.

This may sound confusing at first, but it is easier in practice. The goal is to remove yourself from the experience (the scene on the screen) and allow the part of you that is close to the situation, the one that would speak about it to a friend and tell of the anger and humiliation (the you in the theater) to sit away from the screen or experience. The fact that there is another "you" in the projection booth removes the necessity and power of observation and comment from that "closer you" who is sitting in the theater. The "you" in the projection booth is now quite objective, more in control, and less likely to succumb to the program's power.

This exercise really works, quickly and well. A key ingredient, however, is to position yourself as we have described. It is important to become objective and removed from the power of the moment to be able to change the structure of the program. And it may take a little practice to do this positioning in the exercise. You can start by practicing a different perspective right now. As you are reading this book, imagine yourself watching yourself read the book from across the room. When you can do that, imagine another "you" peeking in the window, watching "you" watch you read the book.

As we continue with the exercise, remember, the goal is to change the structure of the program at the subconscious level. And the subconscious level is relating to—and having a response about—visual, auditory or kinesthetic input, not necessarily the content. So, what we do now is have fun with the movie and change all the aspects of the visual, auditory and kinesthetic ingredients.

Let the movie run through. Now run it again with changes. If it was in color, change it to black and white. If the sound was soft, make it loud. If the people in the scenes are close up, make them far away. Run the movie backwards. Make the "actors" speak gibberish and put subtitles in the movie. Change ***anything*** you can think of. Make the people in the movie animals or giants or midgets. Have the patrolman riding a bike. Let the movie become a series of snapshots, and let them come up on the screen in random sequence.

What you are doing is disrupting the conditioned response pattern as well as the sequence of the program's elements. In essence, you are learning to view the scene in a different way which simply allows you freedom from a program's power. It allows you to make a choice about the situation rather than defaulting into what you are pre-programmed to feel and do.

And, here's some good news. Remember the principle about the subconscious mind dealing with dynamics not content? And remember how everything you experience fits into the dynamics of one or more of the nine programming areas in our model? This highway patrolman illustration may be unique in content (the road you are driving on, the city where you live), but it is not unique in dynamics.

When you change the power of the program regarding this situation, it can help change the power of the program in all situations that have the same dynamic. That is not to say that you cannot or should not use this exercise and method to deal with other life situations. But it is to say that the more you do this, the more you get cumulative effect. Changing one area of your life has a ripple effect in other aspects of your life. You can't become more positive in dealing with one authority figure without it helping your ability to deal with all authority figures.

Once you have done this exercise, maybe repeatedly, you will find your automatic response changing when it comes to the situation in question. This simply allows you the freedom to look at the situation differently and make a choice about your attitude and behavior. You still may deserve the ticket.

So, method one stops the power of the program by bathing it with truth. Method two stops the power of the program by changing its structure, thus changing the outcome or your response. Both methods employ the components of detection (what is the program), a method for confronting the program then choice about what you want to believe and do.

If you've tried the first two methods and you still find a program has power, you can use our third method. This third method is designed to actually reprogram your subconscious mind. It takes what is happening already, acknowledges it, makes a choice about what you want then trains your subconscious mind to automatically respond in the way you *want* to rather than the way your previously dysfunctional program dictated that you would.

This third method of reprogramming involves a seven-step process. This book will teach you the essence of the steps and you will realize the power of the process. Another one of our books that is solely focused on this process teaches you every aspect, reason and nuance of meaning and application about each step. Understanding all of that is great, but simply understanding the steps and how to implement them is sufficient to receive the incredible results of this process. In addition to reprogramming specific programs, people have used this seven-step process to lose weight, become a better athlete, develop more confidence in life and get rid of a multitude of unwanted habits, attitudes or behaviors.

Step One: Own the problem.

It is probably obvious to you by now. If you aren't aware of something, you can't change it. Additionally, even if you are aware of it, if you don't own it, you can't change it. If you wallow in self-pity, blaming life or another person for your problems, you have subtly shifted responsibility for your problems to the person or situation you are blaming.

It is important to intimately know what you want to change. Understand it as much as possible, the reason it exists, how it has served you in the past. In short, understand where and why your program started.

Beyond awareness and understanding, it is important that you accept and take responsibility for the problem or the program you want to change. You are not taking responsibility for its beginning, just its current results and consequences, how it is affecting you today.

Step Two: Choose a specific desired outcome.

After you understand and own the problem or program you want to change, you begin to be in control. And, now that you are, you can choose what you want your attitude, behavior or response to be. No longer are you under the control of a pre-programmed response.

Sometimes a response has become so familiar and even comfortable that you don't know how to choose a different response. If this is how it is with you, ask yourself this question, "What would it be like to *not* have the problem or program?" The answer to this question can help you notice how you would be with a different perspective and response.

Be specific about your choice, as specific as possible. Don't choose, "I want to be a better father," rather, choose, "I choose to spend two days a week in quality time with my children." It is better to choose, "I choose to be calm and objective, listening carefully and responding politely when I am in the presence of an authority figure," rather than, "I want to be stronger in the presence of an authority figure," or "I'm not going to lose my cool when with a policeman."

Specificity and clarity help you be more focused. They help you implement the other aspects of this process by giving something specific to focus on. Further, they help you recognize when you are successful. It is harder to measure "fluffy" goals. It is easier, for example, to determine whether you were "calm, listening carefully and responding politely," than if you "didn't lose your cool."

Step Three: Visualize the new you as a present reality.

Two of the ways to access your subconscious mind are through relaxation and visualization; this step uses both. Specifically, you are to imagine your choice in the previous step is a reality and practice visualizing it clearly at least five times a day during a state of relaxation. It is helpful and important to use your three dominant sensory modes—the senses you use most to remember and process information. Those senses are the same ones we talked about in method two, visual, auditory and kinesthetic.

Take a deep breath. Relax your body. Maybe close your eyes. After you do this, imagine the new you with your choice a reality. See it clearly. Imagine yourself standing in the presence of the patrolman calm and engaged. Notice what it looks like. See all the colors and shapes clearly. Now step into the scene and feel what it is like to be in your body that is in that scene. Notice what your body feels and how peaceful your emotions are. Now use the auditory mode by verbally affirming this new you. Use present tense, positive affirmations: "I am calm. I am confident. I feel good. I listen carefully and clearly. I am..."

It is important to see the scene, feel what it is like and verbally affirm—all in the present tense. You are retraining your subconscious mind to see this as a reality. If you see it as a future reality, "I *will* be calm," that statement says that you aren't calm now. It also gives you a different calibration point as you live life.

Through this process you are calibrating about the reality that is in you, the reality of your choice, *not* the reality of your past inertia and program. If you are trying to lose weight, for instance, and you are 180 pounds trying to get to 150, there is a major difference to your subconscious mind in seeing yourself as a 180 pound person trying to get to 150 pounds, or seeing yourself as a 150 pound person with 30 extra pounds. What you see is what you get. Your calibration point becomes the reality that the rest of your life rallies around. It is no different than the set point theory in weight loss.

So, five times a day, practice this visualization. When you wake up and just before you go to sleep are good times. At other times, simply stop, relax, and do the visualization exercise. It doesn't have to take long. You can do it in a minute or two.

Step Four: Create a reminder of your chosen response.

Step three involves a conscious choice to visualize your chosen response. Step four is a way of continuously reminding you of your chosen response in a conditioned response way.

We are products of conditioned responses everyday through advertising. We're sure you can finish the phrase, "You deserve a break to day at ______." In fact you are probably singing the tune in your mind as you say the words. The phrase becomes the "condition" that automatically, without choice, results in the response of "McDonalds." A program? Yes it is!

Step four says you do that for yourself in regards to your new chosen response. The conditioned response is called an "anchor." In other words, the response is "anchored" to the condition of "whatever." And it truly can be "whatever." We have had people anchor a response to their watch, to a post-it note, to the refrigerator handle, to Avery™ dots; anything can work. The key is to use something you will be encountering regularly. Many people have used something they can carry in their pocket or place on their desk.

How you anchor a response is to repeatedly do the visualization exercise while looking at and touching your anchor. If it is a stone you are going to place in your pocket, hold the stone and focus on it. As you see the color of the stone and feel its texture do the visualization exercise slowly and with deep concentration. Do this a few times throughout the day so the anchoring effect will become stronger. Then, every time you reach into your pocket or purse or see the stone on your desk, your subconscious mind will be reminded of the "you" that is in your visualization exercise—the new you. In effect, this anchoring technique fires off a mini-version of the visualization exercise every time you come in contact with your anchor. This compounds the positive effect of the conscious visualization process in step three.

Step Five: Successfully accomplish a small task daily.

The psychology behind this step is to give you an experience of success along with a measurement of the success of the seven-step process. Plus, its fun.

Choose something that you enjoy, something that can be done in small steps, something that doesn't take much time, something that you can do everyday and see the results of, and something that is different than what you are trying to change or reprogram. If you like to work in your garden; choose this, "I will pull three weeds a day," or "I will fluff up the soil around five plants a day." If you have a hobby, choose to do something small with that hobby every day. If you are a spiritual person, you can choose to memorize a small portion of scripture or some other writing.

As you do this step, you learn a greater degree of self-discipline, you get a diversion that is fun, you prove to your subconscious that you can be successful, and you create a measuring stick of success. The more weeds that get pulled, the more you have practiced this seven-step process. You get to tangibly see progress on a daily basis.

Step Six: Ask a "coach" to hold you accountable.

We do better when someone is encouraging us. And, let's face it, we do better when someone is holding us accountable. That's what this step is all about.

Choose someone other than those who live with you, and preferably someone other than your family members to be an accountability coach. This person does not have to know how to do what you are doing; they don't have to be knowledgeable of the skills you need for success, and they should not take responsibility for your process. You must always maintain responsibility for yourself!

You are to simply ask this person to call you or check in with you about your process as often as you need—once a week, once a day—whatever you think you need. The role of this person is simply to ask you if you are doing your exercises. The role does not include nagging, asking for reasons why you didn't, or anything like that. The role is simply one of a caring human being who is going to check in to let you report on your activity and progress.

Step Seven: Have a winning attitude connected to a Higher Power

This step has to do with your attitude and perspective. The attitude is one that believes you cannot fail. And, indeed, you cannot fail at this process. You can start the process, and you can stop it, but you cannot fail at it. How is that true? Because of a principle you learned earlier in this book. Everything is input.

If you are going to drive from San Francisco, California to Miami, Florida, yet after a day of driving you see the city limit sign for Seattle, have you failed? Nope! You are definitely going the wrong way. In fact, you are going just about as wrong a way as you can. But you have not failed. The sign simply says you need to adjust your direction.

Let us say that you decide you want to drive from California to Miami. You can zigzag all across our nation, but you cannot fail at getting to Miami if you take everything along the way as input. You can even choose to stop and stay in Texas if you want. The process never takes away your power of choice. But your attitude can be one of winning since you cannot fail.

Don't put unrealistic timelines on yourself, however. To lose 50 pounds in two days, to drive to Miami in two hours, to change a program by this afternoon, all may be unrealistic. Let time take its natural course. And, typically, you will get results faster than you realize. But if you are focused on the time element, you really aren't focused on the real change goal. Remember to treat everything as input as you keep your eye on your goal.

The part about connection with a Higher Power is the cosmic connection in this process. You are not alone, and obviously, there are different belief systems when it comes to this part. For us it is God. Use whatever Higher Power you believe in. Just recognize that you have access to and are supported by a power bigger than yourself.

Using one or more of the three methods in this chapter will help you manage or change your programs with the ultimate goal of your being in control of your programs not them in control of you.

By now, with the understandings and the tools in the previous chapters, you are probably feeling pretty good. You understand what makes you tick. You know how and why you do what you do. You have a way to change your unwanted attitudes, behaviors, and the response of your auto-programs. What's left?

If you are like most people you might be experiencing an awareness of some "stuff" you have been carrying for a long time, some hurts, regrets, sorrows, anger, or pain of some sort. You may also be feeling a bit of loss. You may even feel a little off balance. The next chapter will teach you how to completely cleanse of your stored baggage. We will teach you how to go through a process of loss that inevitably comes with any change—even change for the better. And we will teach you how to have and maintain a life of balance.

Meanwhile, congratulations for making it this far! All along we have been eager to bring you through the entire process because we have seen the end of the story so many times and want you to experience it, too. We have seen the success people have, and we have had such great joy in watching them find their true selves and become free to live life by choice.

But typically, at this point, people know they are free in truth but they don't feel completely free. It is because total freedom can only come when you are free ***to*** be who you are ***and*** free ***from*** what you have been. This involves getting rid of all the hurts and pains you carry that have been a part of the programs you have been so intimate with for so many years. It involves a cleansing process and possibly a grieving process.

You've made it out of the muddy swamps your programs were bred in. You now stand in the light of freedom and truth. You are ready to run—but you are aware of the dried and caked mud that covers your free spirit. So we're going to show you how to be free from that too—now. So hurry—turn the page and get totally and completely free. It's time for a bath.

Chapter 8

Living in Balance

...And getting rid of stored baggage and feelings of loss.

You would think he was silly, childish, ridiculous, or just plain crazy. We know otherwise, but let's set up the scene.

James sat in the recliner in our living room. He was attending an advanced Personal Growth Intensive. He knew about programs, where they came from, how they affected him and how to manage or reprogram them. He had practiced the knowledge quite well. People around him positively commented on his change and growth.

University educated, he managed and led 40 people in his company. He was liked and listened to. He was successful but still had a secret.

As is true with most people who become free to live their life on choice, James had some baggage. Even though we know where our programs come from, that knowledge doesn't take away the sorrow and loss, the hurt and rejections, the feelings that are associated with our past. Do you know what we are talking about?

Earlier in this book, when we talked about our DPI we did it without blame. Instead, because we understand the principles of life we understand where our parents were coming from. We can then turn and give unconditional acceptance and understanding to the DPI who taught us conditional acceptance. Just like us, our parents made the best choice available to them. Nevertheless, the pain of rejection is still real when we get the message that we are not acceptable because we didn't do things right or good enough.

The experience of having to grow up too fast, for example, and be the child-parent who was responsible for everyone else's well being carries with it regret and feelings of loss. You never got to be a kid and experience the carefree fun of childhood. And you can feel deeply sad about that.

So, most people carry baggage. And often, that baggage is associated with a particular experience, an experience that stands symbolic of life because it has the dynamics of what you constantly experience in life. That's what James found as he sat in our chair.

The baggage he carried was, indeed, loss of childhood and constantly having to do things "right" to be accepted. Having to be responsible for the family and act like an adult even though he was very young, along with feeling constant fear, wondering if he was performing well enough were all a tremendous weight for him to bear.

The experience that epitomized James's life experience took place when his brother was born. James was about six years old. When his brother was brought home from the hospital, his parents moved James out of his bed so his brother could have it. Along with that move he was told, "You're a big boy now," which began the message and meaning of his life script.

The major blow came when his parents took away his favorite pillow to give it to his brother. James loved that pillow. It was his for as far back as he could remember. He had always slept on that pillow. It was his comfort, his peace. And they took it away because, "He was a big boy now."

The rest of us in the room looked at James and felt the depth of his sobs as he related this experience. And his sobs were deep, groaning, grieving, from-the-gut sobs. His body rocked and convulsed with pulsating pain. And all he could say, over and over, was, "They took my pillow. They took my pillow."

Without understanding the story and the dynamics, this educated, professional adult would appear to be making a fool of himself. But when you do understand the dynamics, you sympathize ***and*** you can relate. It seems like all of us carry baggage of some kind, pain that can find its voice in the symbolism of an early childhood experience. For James it was wrapped up in his pillow.

How about you? As you have been practicing the principles of this book, have you become aware of pain that you carry?

Typically, almost always, a person needs to deal with the resulting pain they carry from their relationship with their conditionally accepting DPI. And, though redundant, we remind you that we are not blaming. The pain you carry is simply a cause and effect occurrence. If someone happens to trip and step on your toe, they didn't mean to do it, but it still hurts. Further, you can be sure your parent was carrying pain too.

So, our goal is not to understand our parent's pain or even see our pain as caused by them. Rather it is to own our pain as a natural result of a cause and effect relationship that undoubtedly transcends your parent's relationship with you and flows backwards in time through a multitude of generations, all experiencing the same dynamics because they knew no different. You, however, are free and can now deal with your pain to cleansing and closure.

We taught James a process in his first PGI that he used again in the advanced Personal Growth Intensive. It's a process that works and has been extremely successful in helping people rid themselves of the baggage they carry. The process works for *any* baggage: stored hurts, harbored pain, fearful memories, angry jealousies, anything you know you are carrying.

Our cleansing process is simple, and you have probably seen the elements or steps before. The magic in the process is using all three steps in it. Other processes suggest one or two but we have found you must use all three components of this cleansing process to be successful and truly experience complete cleansing.

The three components or steps to the cleansing process are:

1. Write and feel
2. Read and feel
3. Perform a symbolic ceremony of closure

The first step, "Write and feel," is about getting everything that is inside, outside. It involves finding some quiet time to yourself and writing down everything that is in your mind about the hurt, pain or loss you are carrying.

The goal of step one is not to create a great literary writing piece, nor is it to write ***to*** someone. The writing is not something you are going to keep, and, even though your "letter" may be addressed to someone, it will never be given to that person. So the goal is not to write for or to someone else, rather, it is to put on paper ***everything*** that comes to your mind about the baggage you are carrying.

For example, James may focus on the situation where his parents took away his pillow, that moment of experience that symbolized his life script and how he lived the rest of his life until he understood what was going on. He would begin his letter with, "Dear Mom and Dad," then whatever his mind gave him next he would write down.

Notice an important distinction here. James is not writing *to* his Mom and Dad; they are just the focal point of his writing. Nor is he necessarily writing *about* the situation. He is allowing his mind to give him whatever comes. And that is what he writes down. If he begins a sentence and his mind jumps to something else, that's ok. He writes whatever comes. If he feels like scribbling on the paper, he does that. The sentences may not make sense, that's ok too. This is not a literary exercise, it is simply getting everything inside, outside.

The words James writes may not make sense. They may not be polite. They may not be logical. They may be a string of curse words he would never say out loud. If it is in his mind—*it is in his mind!* This is what cleansing is about, getting rid of the stuff that is there.

So James writes. And writes. And writes. How long? (You'll love this). We tell people, "You will know you are done when you are done." And it's true. You keep writing until your mind gives you nothing else to write. And to be sure that there is nothing more, when you are finished, sit for a few minutes and listen to your inner self. If something else comes to you, write it down.

This first step can be likened to cutting off the top of an ice berg. You can't see what is under the water, but you know there is a lot there. So you lop off the top. What happens? Of course, more floats up. You lop that off too. What happens? More floats up. As you keep doing this, more and more ice floats to the surface until there is no more ice. You know you are done when you are done.

You may even be surprised with what comes up. That's normal. Almost like an observer, you continue to allow thoughts, feelings, and words to come up. You may begin writing words and sentences that are directly from the little boy or little girl that is in you from the perspective of the child that experienced the hurt or pain. *Whatever* comes, write it down. DO NOT EDIT! If you do, you are not cleansing what is stored inside. Instead you will undoubtedly begin using the coping concepts you have used all your life to get by.

Our first step says, "Write *and feel.*" It is important to allow yourself to feel while you are writing. No matter what they are, allow your emotions out. If you feel like crying because of deep hurt and pain, do it. If you feel anger, express it, safely (yell, go for a brisk walk, hit a soft cushion). If you feel sad, allow yourself to let the tears of sadness flow.

The key here is to *allow* whatever words or feelings that come to you to be expressed, the words on paper, the feelings in your body. Do not *make* anything happen. Do not force yourself to try and feel something because you think you are supposed to. This is an exercise in freedom to be whoever you are, freedom to express whatever is there. You are giving yourself unconditional acceptance as you observe and capture the thoughts and feelings from stored experience.

Do the first step completely. And do it in one sitting. Carve out some time for you to do this in private and *allow* yourself to be honest, real, genuine—not hiding anything from yourself, which is a real irony. If it is in there, it is in there. Hiding from yourself is only a game of hide and seek where the hider and the seeker both know where the other one is. They just refuse to acknowledge it. Silly, right? So be yourself and let yourself be.

For your cleansing letter, focus on a situation or a stored feeling, notice who is associated with that situation or feeling, then begin writing to that person. If another person comes to mind as you are writing, go ahead and write to that person too. Just go with whatever comes up. Simply start by writing to the person who is mostly associated with your hurt, pain or anger. And if you don't know who to begin writing to, try writing to your DPI. Start with, "Dear (Mom or Dad)," and let your mind give you whatever comes. Then write it and express the emotions connected with your writing.

Fairly soon after you have done step one "Write and feel," do step two. It is best if you can do it the same day. The first two steps are vital to the cleansing process. Don't shrink from them.

Step two is to "Read and feel." This involves another person, a person who is safe, one who will not judge you or try to "fix" you. Choose someone whom you can trust to simply be there as you read the letter you have written. But before you go off and read it to them, let us explain the dynamics of this second step.

Emotion, especially negative emotion, needs to be expressed for it to be released. In fact, if it is not expressed, it still tends to come out in inappropriate ways. Sickness, stress, other bodily manifestations as well as inappropriate responses to others, all can be ways unexpressed emotion seeps out.

Writing about your feelings is not sufficient for expression. That's why we have talked to many people who have tried the "write it on paper then throw it away" technique and found it doesn't work. The writing, in step one, is designed to capture what is there and can even serve to put what's there in a better perspective. Writing about what's inside you has the same dynamics as when you tell someone about a nightmare. Before you tell them it can seem overwhelmingly powerful. As you speak about it, some of the power of the nightmare dissipates. But capturing your inner thoughts and feelings on paper, though it may serve to diminish the power of the baggage through better perspective, will still not be sufficient for complete cleansing.

In order for you to be fully free of stored baggage, you must express it to another human being. Even those who are spiritual find that they have a need for two types of relationships, a vertical one (connected to a Higher Power) and a horizontal one (connections with other humans). An illustration from scripture may help.

In Genesis, the first book of the Bible, there is the story of God creating Adam and Eve. But God creates Adam first after he has created everything else including the animals. So we find Adam, in the very presence of God, living in a perfect world with every need met, turning to God and saying, "Where is someone for me?" The story illustrates that, even in a perfect world connected with God, there is incompletion without another human being to relate to.

We believe this is another reason why some people have stored baggage and can't get rid of it—they believe they *should* be rid of it because they took it to God. But that is not how God made us in the first place. Certainly God can give us peace, understanding and support. But, short of miracles, God, too, plays by the rules—the rules of cause and effect. If you break your arm, there are certain things you do for healing. You don't just pray about it. You also need a cast. When you have emotional baggage, one aspect of the cause and effect process is to express that emotion to another human being.

So step two, no matter how seemingly uncomfortable, is necessary for cleansing. Find someone who will be the person who will listen to you. Allow yourself to feel in their presence. Tears are often associated with cleansing. That person needs to be ok with that and not feel like they need to stop you or fix the problem. This is simply a cleansing process and your friend's presence is a part of it. There is nothing more for your friend to do than listen supportively and be genuinely sympathetic.

We would like to emphasize the importance of you allowing yourself freedom of expression during the reading. Whatever you feel, allow yourself to feel it and express it. And take your time. If you need silence for a while before reading the next sentence, that's ok. If you need to sob for fifteen minutes, that's ok, too. Tell your friend to simply be patient and accepting during your reading. This person is to simply receive whatever you express.

One word of caution. Make sure you choose someone who will not carry your baggage. If your baggage is about your mom, for instance, and you choose your dad to receive your reading, he may then have to carry what you have said about your mom in his mind. This would not be fair. Choose a neutral person who is not connected to the person you have focused on in your writing. Don't choose a fellow employee, for example, to listen to you read a cleansing letter about your mutual supervisor. This can create doubts or questions in your fellow employee's mind. And, again, this is not fair because you are writing about *your* experience, which is primarily coming from *your* perspective, which is derived from *your* programs. Your fellow employee can have a totally different perspective, experience and relationship with your supervisor. So choose someone safe: someone who is supportive, accepting, neutral and non-connected to the persons or issues in your letter.

We have seen all kinds of experiences from people we have helped do this. Some people write their cleansing letter and feel nothing. Then in reading it, a rush of emotions emerges. Others experience a tremendous amount of deep emotions during the writing and find the reading to almost be a joyous and freeing experience without much emotion at all. And, of course, there are varying experiences within the spectrum of the above two illustrations. There is no right or wrong way to experience this. There is just your way. Allow it to happen!

Once you have finished steps one and two, you will undoubtedly experience the cleansing you are looking for. But it will not be complete without step three "Perform a symbolic ceremony of closure." It comes after you complete step two, but it may not come right after. Often people want to do step three immediately. Others wait (and we'll tell you what to wait for). The key is to sense that you are truly done, free and have no more stored baggage. We'll explain the step then tell you what to wait for, when to do your ceremony.

Surrounding every major event in any culture there is ceremony. We have holidays that commemorate and celebrate something such as New Year's Day. We have weddings, bar mitzvahs, graduations, funerals, initiations, all to remember, celebrate and bring one chapter of our life to a close so as to begin another. Ceremony is not necessary from a logical point of view, but it is as old as the first human cultures and have always been used for specific benefit.

The benefits of ceremony are to bring closure to what has gone before, to create a benchmark that clearly defines an ending and beginning point, to inaugurate something new, and to change our mindset. In a culture that has a rite of passage that a young boy goes through to become a man, what changes? If the ceremony is a day long, is the boy (who is now a "man") a different person? Have his talents, abilities, size or any other aspect about his person changed in this day of ceremony? No. So what has changed? It is his mind, his perspective. Now he is a man, so says the ceremony, so he sees things differently and acts the way a man would act. The ceremony has changed his mindset along with the resulting perception and behavior.

People who live together then get married report a difference. Nothing really changes on the outside. But even if the couple has been living together for years, the mindset changes with the ceremony, and that has a subtle, yet powerful influence on the relationship. Perspective changes and so does behavior.

This is the kind of dynamic we are talking about in performing a ceremony of closure for this cleansing process. When you do a ceremony about your cleansing, you release the old, benchmark your choice to move on and let the past go. You begin living without the baggage, and you change your mindset about the hurt or pain you have been carrying.

The ceremony involves your getting rid of your cleansing letter in a symbolic way. You can burn it, flush it down the toilet, or bury it. One person actually buried theirs with other symbolic items that represented what they were cleansing from. Another person buried his at the headwaters of a river to symbolize it being left in the dust while the waters of his new life flowed on from this place. We have had people come up with all kinds of creative ways to dispose of the letter. One person climbed to the top of a mountain, tore the letter up into little pieces, then let the wind blow it away. (He made sure he had biodegradable paper). Still another person tore his letter up and threw it into a waterfall.

The key is to choose something that is symbolic and meaningful for you. Another important ingredient to this cleansing ceremony is to have one or more witnesses. As you think about most of our ceremonies, they need to have witnesses to make them meaningful, legal or binding. Even those that don't, like New Year's Day, are made more meaningful or significant with at least one other person there. So choose someone to be with you during your ceremony.

A funny story happened to my, Bill's, sister when she did this process. She wanted to hike to a special lake in the mountains and burn her letter there. But she couldn't get anyone to go with her during the only time she was going to be close to this mountain lake to perform her ceremony. Creatively, she took her video camera and taped her ceremony so she could show others later. Though meaningful, it was quite funny to watch her on the video while she spoke of how proud of herself she was and said other things a "witness" might say if present. She played both roles quite nicely.

When you have your ceremony, it is important to reiterate your choices about this cleansing process. Speak to the person who is witnessing this event. Tell them briefly about what you are doing. This will also serve as a benchmarking statement for yourself, something like, "I have been carrying the pain of rejection I felt from my mother for a long time. I now understand where it came from and have completely expressed what I feel about it. This letter represents my expression. As I dispose of it I choose to no longer let the contents of this letter bother me again. I choose to forgive and move on. I choose to be free of this pain. I choose to not carry this pain into other relationships. And from this moment forward, I will live in freedom. Though I may remember the pain and shed a tear of memory, I no longer have the deep, sobbing tears of baggage. This pain will no longer be in control of my life. I choose to let it go."

And you will be able to completely and freely give that message and decision because of the first two steps. When you do those two steps completely, you will find the cleansing that matches the message we are suggesting. And, from our own experience we know, after this cleansing process, though you may have moments of sadness, or even cry a bit as you recall the loss of your childhood or remember the pain you experienced in your past—a remembered tear that you shed is far different than a stored tear. You will learn from experience what we mean.

The above paragraphs explain why you do a ceremony and what is done at the ceremony. But when do you do it? Basically you'll know when you're ready—when you are ready. You will have a clear sense that it is time. It can be immediately after step two or even a few weeks after step two. Don't wait longer than a few weeks, however. If you have waited longer than four to six weeks, it may be that the power of the moment was lost.

What can happen is this: A person experiences the freedom from steps one and two (and there is a tremendous amount of freedom you will feel just by doing these steps), but waits until just the right time or situation to do the ceremony. Then living life creeps in to the picture and they get busy. They forget or just don't get around to doing the ceremony. When we have talked to people who have done this, they seem to have a sense of incompletion. So don't wait too long. And, if six weeks has gone by and you haven't done it, do it anyway, right then.

One of the main reasons people need to wait a bit is to let the feelings they have cleansed about seep out completely. This is done through a process of loss that we can be proactive about managing.

The process of loss is something everyone goes through no matter how healthy a person is. Even if you are moving to something better, you will still have this sense of loss. Have you ever sold a car that you've had for a long time, you know, *finally* gotten rid of that piece of junk? Remember how you felt as the person who bought it drove away? That was a form of loss.

The theory is this: You experience loss within *every* transition in life—an actual loss or a transition to something better. A missed phone call, a promotion, losing a valuable item, having a loved one die—all would qualify for the process of loss. The difference is in the length of time it takes to go through the process of loss and the depth of intensity with which it is experienced. A missed phone call would take a short time to go through and would have fairly shallow feelings. The process of loss associated with the death of a loved one can take a long time to go through and have deep and intense feelings associated with it.

Regardless of the duration and intensity of the process, there are always three stages of loss to go through. They are:

1. Shock and/or denial
2. Anger and/or depression
3. Acceptance and/or understanding

You are probably quite familiar with the first stage. You can't believe it has happened, you are paralyzed in a state of shock. Or, you flat out deny that it has happened. There is a period of time before the reality sinks in that loss has occurred. That time is determined by the kind of loss you are experiencing. Once again, compare the missed phone call to the death of a loved one. And, remember, this can happen with *any* loss, even loss surrounding something you didn't want in the first place. You will experience this first stage even if you are promoted to the position you longed for all your life.

The second stage is anger and/or depression. Depending on the type of loss, anger can range from a constant sense of mild frustration to all out rage. Depression can range from a constant sense of mild sadness or unhappiness to clinical, bed-ridden depression. How you perceive the loss determines the reaction.

We both can remember experiencing this sadness associated with pure loss. We have even experienced it when we received or were experiencing something better in life. And, when you are experiencing this "anger and/or depression" associated with transitioning to something better, it is confusing.

Be careful not to project these feelings onto someone who doesn't deserve it. These feelings associated with loss can be diffused, inexplicable and mysterious, so we try and find a home for them. Often we will look around us and find a likely candidate for our feelings and say, "It must be you (husband, wife, child, boss, friend) who is causing me this anger or sadness," and react to them accordingly.

Try to understand your feelings for what they are. You are not angry or depressed because someone did something to you. Recognize that your feelings that are associated with this process of loss are simply because of loss. Don't give them an inappropriate "home."

This brings up the point about what to do with these feelings. First of all, recognize that you can't run from the feelings, you can't get around them, you can't ignore them—you have to go through them. And going through them simply means expressing them to a safe person.

Remember, emotions need to be expressed. Anything short of that is going to result in building up more baggage. So, with all aspects of this process of loss, express what you are feeling. Express the shock or denial as well as the anger or depression. Then you can move yourself through the loss. Some people who do not express themselves can get stuck in a stage for the rest of their life. Have you seen a person who is chronically depressed or sad? Have you seen a person who is continuously angry at the world for no apparent reason? One reason for this is the person might be stuck in stage two of loss and is refusing to face the loss or express the feelings associated with it.

The third stage, "acceptance and/or understanding" is when you finally are able to at least accept the loss and possibly even understand it. Though you may not be able to understand why something happened, you will at least come to the place where you can accept it and move on in freedom.

This process of loss is quite fluid. It does not have clean, clear transition points. You can move back and forth between the two "and/or" characteristics of a certain stage and you can move up and down the process as well. You may think you are through with shock and/or denial when you wake up one morning and have an hour or two of, "Did this really happen" again. You may feel like you have come to accept what has happened but find yourself once again overwhelmed with grief or sadness again.

The key is to do exactly what the old phrase says, "Go with the flow." Don't fight the process, allow it to happen. Express yourself as each stage emerges. And if you do this you will walk gently through the process of loss to its completion.

Though this process of loss is something we all experience associated with many things (even the kind of growth you are learning about in this book), you can fairly well count on the fact that you will experience loss as you do the cleansing process. Most of the time it occurs before the ceremony in step three but sometimes it is after that. Sometimes it occurs rather dramatically and quickly as you are doing steps one and two. There is no clear rule as to when it will occur; just deal with it as we have described whenever you experience loss.

If you have something you need to cleanse from or if you need to complete a process of loss and you have not done one or both of these you will undoubtedly feel off balance. But even when you take care of these issues you may still not feel balanced. If this happens to you, it is probably because you are not fulfilling the seven areas of life necessary for balance. We will teach you about those areas next, but first a bit of review to ramp up to them.

The basic principles you have learned in this book are the scientific principles that determine how you become programmed. Based on that learning, you can know what makes you the way you are. The basic programming model tells you how your life will be lived, what your programs are and how they affect your perspective, attitude, behavior and responses. That learning helps you understand yourself completely.

By now, you have found your programs, tested them to see which ones are working for you and which ones are not, learned how to manage or reprogram your dysfunctional programs, and you have cleansed from stored baggage. The next model tells you *where* you live out your programs.

There are seven areas or categories within which you live life. We'll list them with bullets, and haven't numbered them because each one has as much importance as another. There is no ranking in this list, and there is no prioritization. The seven areas of life within which you are continuously living are:

- Mental
- Physical
- Spiritual
- Relational
- Emotional
- Professional
- Recreational

Every one of your programs will be lived out in one or more areas of this list. We'll tell you what we mean by each item on the list.

Mental: *What gives you mental challenge, what stimulates your mind.*

Spiritual: *The area of life wherein you live out your spiritual beliefs; this can be within the context of religion solely, your connection with a sense of beauty and nature, your connection with life as a whole.*

Physical: *Anything that has to do with your physical well-being—from nutrition to exercise.*

Relational: *Anything that has to do with your relationships with other people from family to friendship to community; the distinction here is relationships with* <u>*people*</u> *not with events, tasks, functions or work.*

Emotional: *The ability to be in touch with and express your emotions.*

Professional: *What you do for your work or profession, not necessarily only what you get paid for; this is the place where you exercise your work related or professional related talents.*

Recreational: *Where you re-create yourself; what you do for fun and diversions.*

Every one of these areas must be fulfilled for you to feel in balance. But no one can tell you how to fulfill them. Fulfillment is a completely subjective criterion. We know of one person that has to read multiple books a week to have their mental area of life fulfilled. We know of another person who doesn't read at all but watches a news magazine television show once a week to fulfill the need for mental stimulation and challenge. These two people are quite different yet each has *their own* criteria for fulfillment. If the first person read very few books in a week there would not be fulfillment. Nor could the second person read books to feel fulfilled. We have to follow *our own* subjective criteria for fulfillment.

You may ask, "Where does our criterion come from?" It comes through the same process that our programs come from.

In essence, you have "program-like" dynamics that surround your criteria. If you use the same processes we talked about in chapter six on finding your programs, you can begin to understand where your criteria came from.

What is more important, however, is understanding *what* your criteria are more than *where* they come from. Certainly, you can change your criteria by choice anytime you want. But the crucial concept here is this: If any one of these areas is not fulfilled, you will feel out of balance in *all* areas.

The president of an architectural firm in Dallas, Texas spoke about feeling out of balance. As he did the analysis we will show you shortly, he found that two of the areas were not being fulfilled, his spiritual and relational areas. To fulfill his spiritual area, he needed to go to church at least once a month. To fulfill his relational area, he needed to connect with his immediate family once a week. He was doing neither.

Before he knew which areas were not being fulfilled, he felt out of balance in *all* of the areas. When he knew where the source of imbalance was, he felt somewhat more in balance. Then when he made a plan to go to church once a month and call his relatives once a week, he felt in balance again. This is part of the irony of this model. If you simply *make a definitive plan*, even if you are not able to follow through yet, you will immediately feel back in balance.

The dynamic that is at work here has to do with control. When life's preoccupations, such as work, crises or other intrusions, erode away what we would typically do to feel in balance, something else is in control. We are not in control of our life, the preoccupations are. So we feel out of balance. The minute we make a plan to do something about the lack, we are in control again, and thus feel in balance again. And it really is that simple.

Balance, then, comes from getting rid of the stored baggage that weighs us down, getting completely through loss that inevitably shrouds us now and then, and proactively fulfilling the seven areas within which we live life. Do you recognize where we are?

We are free!

Do you get that?

We are FREE!

YOU ARE FREE!

You understand the basics of human nature. You know what makes you tick. You know how to find and manage your programs. You know how to have balance in life. You are in control of your life; no one else is.

At this point, people want to focus on others. They want to take what they have learned and apply it to, for, or with others. We will tell you what to do in the next chapter when it comes to applying this information to them. Begin to think of everyone with whom you associate that you want to have the same experience you are having. In the next chapter you will have step by step, specific and definitive instruction for what to do.

So go forth, oh free one! Learn the principle that can make others disciples of your freedom. We think you will be pleased and surprised with the content of the next chapter.

Chapter 9

WHAT TO DO WITH OTHERS ...NOW THAT YOU'VE LEARNED AND CHANGED?

Nothing!

Chapter 10

Living with the New You ...What to Expect.

Kevin was excited about his growth. He learned everything in this book and began putting it into practice. He felt free, was free, and wanted everyone around him to experience what he found. He called ahead and told his wife about his freedom and how he had changed. He told her she would see a difference. He told others, too. And he told them all how they could be free, too, if they just practiced what he had learned. He would tell them how. But people tended to resist Kevin's enthusiastic "teaching." Somehow, it felt like scolding.

Todd had a different experience than Kevin. He, too, was free and went home *being* free. He simply lived his freedom, he lived what he learned. No longer did people's criticism cause him to crawl in a hole for a week. He treated it as input and dealt with it to closure. He was more peaceful, objective, and connected with others. He radiated happiness and confidence. And people started to want what Todd had. They asked him about it, and he was able to tell them about *his* experience. Then, if the listener wanted, he was able to tell them where they could learn how to be free, too.

What is the difference between Kevin and Todd? In his excitement Kevin tried to live differently and tell others how to do that. Todd simply was different. He let the changes he had experienced do the "talking" while he went about living his life in freedom.

It is important to understand, the only person you can change is ***you.*** In the last chapter, chapter nine, we told you what you can do to change others. Nothing.

Certainly, you can teach others, *if they want to learn.* You can share your experience, *if they want to listen.* And you can give them this book, *if they want to receive it.* Any attempt to coerce someone into changing, however, even if it is for their best good, will often backfire and actually harden the person so they are resistant to learning in the future.

Do *not* take responsibility for another person's growth. You can't anyway. Live your life and let them be drawn to what they see. The best way to eliminate the darkness in the room is to put a light in it, even a small candle flame will do. You can't eliminate the darkness by focusing on it and somehow trying to get rid of it. Instead, it needs to be replaced with light.

As you live your life, you become a beacon of freedom, a lighthouse on the rocky shores of life. People will be drawn to you. Then, and only then, will you have influence and can teach them. So, for now, focus on *you.* Care about others; love others; interact well with others, but focus on maintaining the new you. That's the best way to influence the people around you.

What can you expect for this new "you?" What is over the horizon for you? What kinds of situations, dynamics, obstacles, or new growth will you find as you walk your life's journey? We will answer some of these questions for you in this chapter. Everyone is unique, but many people have similar experiences as they begin living with their newfound freedom and personal power.

Something you can expect from other people is that they may have a tendency to not let you change. The reason for this comes from systems theory. From solar systems to family systems, systems have a strong inertial force to stay the same. Anything that disrupts the system is unwanted or rejected.

Allergies are an example of this concept. Pollen is seen by the body as an enemy, something that is foreign to our body's system.

To protect itself, the body creates histamines, protective secretions that surround the pollen but they also create watery eyes, an itchy throat and a runny nose. The actual protective mechanism the body uses causes *itself* to be uncomfortable.

This is what happens with a system of people. Whether you are looking at your family system, your work relationship system or the system created with you and your friends—when you change it affects the system.

One way this system dynamic manifests itself is when someone in your "system" does not believe in your change. You may be challenged or questioned, "How can you actually be interested in me (not fearful, able to be confident, not upset when I disagree with you, etc.—all focusing on the old you) after so many years of you being a different way?" You can even hear, "Who do you think you are? How can you think you are good enough or strong enough to change?"

Without realizing it, people who challenge or question you and your change are really thinking about themselves. (Remember the principle, *every response is about you*)? They may be feeling fearful or threatened because their system has changed. Further, the old you probably fulfilled some kind of need or served some kind of purpose for them. A dramatic example is the "enabler" or "codependent" in an alcoholic's system. When the alcoholic quits drinking, it affects the people in that system by changing their identity and purpose.

Another way this system dynamic affects others is when you aren't consistent, when you manifest some behavior or attitude that is from the old you. You can be sure people will pounce on that inconsistency. Let's say after your change you no longer lose your temper easily. But one time, an old program fires and you get fairly angry with another person; you will undoubtedly hear, "See, you really haven't changed."

So the people in your system may resist your change and actually try to sabotage it. And they can be quite vocal about it, giving negative or derogatory messages. The problem comes when you begin to believe the negative message. Let us give you a simple illustration to give you perspective on your change. Your change is equivalent to having moved from the United States to New Zealand. You are now surrounded by a new environment—a new you. When you make a mistake or revert back to being the old you for a moment, you are blowing it in New Zealand, you are not back in America. Do not, DO NOT, ***DO NOT*** believe the lie that you have never changed. Who you are is determined by choice that results in behavior and interaction—it is not your behavior and interaction that determine who you are.

The key is to remain as consistent as you can, and when you make a mistake exhibiting the attributes of the old you, own it. Communicate about it and apologize. No matter what others say, give your own clear message, "I'm sorry. I let some of the old me take control for a moment. That's not how I want to be or am going to be. Thank you for your patience with me."

Kathy, one of our PGI graduates, used to be abrasive, abrupt and distant when dealing with others. Her survival programs got in the way of her relating closely to anybody. It took many months for people to believe she had really changed. All the while they were expecting her to be the way she used to be. Many times she got discouraged and wanted to lash out at someone. And, actually, she did sometimes, which only perpetuated the myth that she had not changed.

As Kathy remained consistent in her choice, however, and continued to live out her freedom and power to be the person she wanted to be, her behavior became more consistent, and gradually the people around her stopped resisting her. They finally became able to work with her in a new way. Ironically, what was happening was they had to change to catch up with her change. It's like a dance. When one partner changes the steps, the other partner has to change, too, or the dance can't continue.

Another expectation about this new you is to know that you will have ups and downs in life. Life is not in a stagnate state. It is dynamic, ever-changing. Everything around you changes, grows, flexes and transforms. You will, too. It's normal.

Sometimes, so called "ups and downs" come from feelings; sometimes they come from performance. If you are feeling down because, well, you simply feel down, you tend to put a meaning on it. The feeling can be coming from many sources. Your body functions, a change in the weather, a misunderstanding, a disappointment—all are among the many things that can cause you to have a feeling of some sort. But just because you feel down doesn't mean life is bad.

Feelings do not determine the facts. If you feel like it is Monday but it is Wednesday, your feelings don't change the fact that it is Wednesday. If you feel down, it can also feel like life is going down, too, but what is the fact? What is the truth? Finding the truth will set you free.

Choose to look at reality in the face of your feelings, and determine what is real, what is true, then make choices about the truth. We just talked to a man on the telephone about his leadership and his job. He kept catching himself yielding to false fears, assumptions and the messages of old programs. When he looked at truth, there really wasn't anything to be afraid of; his assumptions were not valid, and his survival programs were not necessary—though they were shouting a pretty loud message. His feelings were no where near the facts.

You can also have a "downer" by not performing a task as best as you can, by making mistakes, or by disappointing someone close to you. Certainly, that can make you feel bad, but it doesn't make you a bad person. You blew it. You may even have consciously made an inappropriate choice for the moment. What do you?

You own the inappropriate choice or inappropriate behavior. You own the fact that you blew it. (Allow the feelings to exist and be expressed. It's ok to feel badly about something without feeling like you are a bad something). Then you learn from the situation, make it as right as you can with the other person or persons involved, then make a choice about *your behavior* while still owning the facts about *your person.* (You are a wonderful and valuable person. You are that because you exist, not because of what you have done or will do, just because you are—*you!)*

Feeling "up" or performing successfully is the mirror image to the above scenario of feeling "down." In both cases everything is input. And it is normal to have ups and downs. It is normal to have success and times of little or no success. Both successful and unsuccessful outcomes are times when you are simply receiving input or feedback. But, remember, it is about how you interacted, behaved or performed, it is not about you as a person. Life is not perfect, but you can manage it as long as you *stay in control* of your perspective and choices.

Something else you can expect as you move forward is that your expectations will change. Imagine this illustration: Tom is married to Nancy. Tom works at a very stressful job that doesn't leave him much time or energy to work around the house. Nancy is a stay-at-home wife who works hard to keep the house clean and comfortable.

Nancy does all the cooking in their house. Every meal, every day, and Nancy is a bit tired of it. Tom and Nancy have received an unexpected windfall of money that lets both of them live at home in a comfortable financial state. Tom, wishing he could have been more helpful around the house before now and thankful for everything that Nancy has done, offers to begin doing all the cooking.

Every day, seven days a week now Tom cooks breakfast, lunch and dinner. Nancy is thankful and happy. After a while, Tom cooking the meals becomes normal. Both of them have settled into the routine. But over time, Tom gets a bit weary of the cooking, too, and presents a new proposal to Nancy.

"How about I cook all the meals five days a week and you cook on the weekends?" "What?" Nancy says. "I have cooked all the meals for so many years and now you want me to cook on the weekends?"

Obviously, this illustration is a bit facetious, but notice something. Go back to the original situation of Tom not cooking at all. Let's say that at that point Tom offers to cook for five days a week, or even just on the weekends for that matter. Nancy would have been thrilled, right? What has happened?

The bar of expectation has risen to new heights. When Tom didn't cook at all, any offer to cook would have been an improvement. When he cooked seven days a week, going back to cooking five days a week (which is five days of cooking more than he used to do) seemed like a backwards step.

The same kind of dynamics happens with you as you grow. The bar of expectation rises to a new level. You now expect more out of yourself and can become discouraged when you don't meet this new expectation. For example, before your change, you might have been pleased if you didn't lose your temper one day out of the week. Now you can be tempted to beat yourself up over having a bit of anger or frustration over someone not following through with a task.

There are two things you can do when this occurs. First, remember history, not in the sense of reliving it but in the sense of remembering where you've come from. Acknowledge and be thankful for the growth you are exhibiting as you compare how you are today with how you used to be. The old adage is true; if you forget your history, you are bound to repeat it.

The second thing to do is to take the current situation at face value and make a choice about it. You are probably just as upset with the frustration you are now experiencing as you were when you lost your temper. Deal with the frustration the same way you dealt with the temper: Find the program, find the truth, re-program the faulty program if necessary, make your choice about how you want to live, and then live out that choice.

And, it's ok to have higher expectations for yourself. Just don't make those expectations be the criteria for your worth or value. Let the higher expectations be your guide and your goal not your jury and your judge.

Here is a situation you may have as you live with the new you: You believe you are free of old programs, you believe you are living your life on choice, yet you find something new about you, some additional problematic program or nuance in how a program is manifested, and when you find this, you wonder if you ever really changed. Consider this next illustration.

Imagine living in a house that is extremely cluttered. It is dirty and there are piles of clothes, boxes and trash everywhere. As you move around in this house, you constantly have to move the boxes (baggage) around to get at this drawer or that cupboard. Over time you have gotten so comfortable with the dirt and clutter, you don't even notice it anymore.

Let's say that you recognize the condition this house is in and you make a decision to clean it up. Through some basic and effective processes you get rid of the boxes and clean up the clutter. Now you live in a clean and organized house. You are thankful, happy and free.

One day, you are walking from the kitchen into the living room and you notice a dirty rag sitting in the hall. Would you say, "Oh my, the house is filthy!" or "See that rag, my house has never been clean in the first place." Neither would occur, right? Right!

Yet we have seen people find some new way a specific program is affecting their life negatively, or they find a new problem behavior or program, something they hadn't noticed before. When they notice either of these, they get discouraged. And usually the discouragement comes from the misconception that once you are free and healthy, you will no longer have problems.

When your house is cluttered and unclean you don't even notice the dirty rag in the hall. It's only after you grow that you can find new levels of understanding. Only then can you find other, more minor problems or programs. When you notice the dirty rag, you have not back slid. You are simply gaining a new learning or revelation. And when you do you deal with it as you did when you found the first major programs and problematic behaviors.

Life is constant growth and learning. You can continue to progress if you use the same principles and tools at every level of awareness or learning. You may find new programs, different ways an old program is manifested, or even greater understanding about an old program. In any case, nothing has changed. If your choice is the same, you can continue to use the same techniques and tools you have already learned to deal with any of your findings. You may need refreshment or reminders of principles, tools and truth at each new level of growth, but refreshment or a reminder is just that. It is not starting over at the base of the mountain.

Here is a bit of "bad" news for some people; your programs may not go away.

There are some people who expect their programs to never raise their ugly head once they have been dealt with. This may be true. But it is also true and more common that often the program will still fire. But even though it fires, you still know how to deal with it so it has no power over you.

Both of us have deep and powerful programs that continue to fire regularly. These programs do not control us, however. Instead we are in control of them. We use the principles and tools in this book to deal with them. And we are able to slay the power of a program in a matter of seconds. You can do it, too, simply by practicing the principles and techniques in this book. We also try to understand patterns or situations that cause our programs to fire. We pay attention to consistent and predictable triggers such as certain thoughts, people or situations. This helps us anticipate a program and deal with it before it can have any power at all.

So, as you go forward living with the new you, these are the types of dynamics you can expect:

- You can expect others to be resistant to, or not understand, your growth.
- You can expect to feel up, and you can expect to feel down.
- You can expect to make mistakes or inappropriate choices.
- You can expect to have a higher level of expectations for yourself.
- You can expect some of your deeper, powerful programs to continue to fire.
- And you can expect to see new areas where you need to grow or change.

The good news is this—the new you has greater, more effective and powerful tools to deal with all of this. Certainly, you have more tools than the old you did. And if any of these expectations or predictions becomes reality, it does not mean you are starting over or have "really not changed." It simply means you are human and are at a new level of growth and interaction. You ***can*** expect to live free and stay free!

There is a story in the Bible about the Children of Israel who were freed from Egyptian slavery. After wandering in the wilderness for forty years because of doubt and disbelief, they came to the borders of their promised land, the land of Canaan.

The story tells how they sent spies into the land who found there were giants inhabiting it. God promised them, however, that they would be victorious in taking the land so they did. And when they removed the giants, the land became theirs.

The Children of Israel were looking for giants when they entered Canaan. It was the giants they had to remove. It was the giants who were their enemies. But let's say that after the land was conquered, a man goes out to the woodpile to get some wood for the fire and encounters a pygmy hiding in the woodpile, a pygmy with the same kind of evil behavior and intent as the giants. That pygmy would have to be dealt with in the same way the giants were; it would just be easier.

The fact that there was a pygmy in the woodpile does not mean the land has not been conquered. Nor does it mean there is some kind of inadequacy on the part of the land owner. It simply means there is something else that needs to be dealt with.

You have left behind the bondage and slavery of old programs controlling you. Maybe you wandered in the wilderness of doubt and disbelief for a time. Then you came to the borders of your promised land. You effectively dealt with the giant programs that controlled you, and you took over your promised land—the place where you are free to be you, living life based on your choice.

As you live with this new you, you can be confident you have driven out the giants in your land. For now don't be too concerned about an occasional pygmy in the woodpile, just deal with the situation as you did your giants.

Oh...one more thing: Do you notice how bright your rainbow shines in this land. The sunlight is bright and pure and the water droplets that create the prism for the rainbow are crystal clear, sparkling like diamonds. Your rainbow is beautiful! But did you know there is a purpose behind every rainbow? That's right. Every rainbow has a purpose that is behind it. What is the purpose for your rainbow? We'll address that question in the next chapter.

Chapter 11

LIVING LIFE FREELY ON PURPOSE ...WITH PURPOSE!

The first rainbow had a message, a meaning—it had purpose.

According to the book of Genesis in the Bible, Noah was asked to build an ark, a boat that would protect anyone who would go on board before the predicted deluge. Evidently, according to some scientists, before Noah's flood, the earth had a different system for watering the world, some kind of firmament greenhouse effect. It did not have rain. When the first rain came then, it was obviously associated with destruction since the great flood, talked about in the history of all cultures on earth, destroyed virtually all of civilization at the time.

When Noah and his family stepped out of the ark after the rains ceased, they saw a rainbow. God knew that it would be a fearful sight since it was connected to the rain that destroyed the earth. To prevent this fear, God connected a meaning to the rainbow saying it would be the symbol of a promise that the world would never be destroyed by a flood again. The rainbow had a purpose.

The purpose of the rainbow is intrinsically linked to the purpose in the situation that creates it. The first rainbow shined through the mist that greeted Noah and his family as a promise of security and peace. There are many situations that have different purposes that can create a rainbow. Imagine these.

There is water splashing around as you ride your car through a car wash listening to the thumping of the thick felt fingers dragging across your car. This water, for the purpose of cleaning your car, can create a rainbow. You see children spraying water from an inner city hydrant on a stiflingly hot day so they can cool down. Their laughter and dancing antics display their pleasure as this splashing water, sprayed for purpose of coolness and pleasure creates a rainbow.

Police in a riot squad spray water to stop an attacking mob and protect the innocent. The jet of water creates a rainbow. A fireman sprays water to stop the destruction of a firestorm and protect a grove of giant sequoias, and as he does his spray creates a rainbow. The purpose of both streams of water is to prevent an attack, one an attack of people, another prevents an attack of fire; both can create a rainbow.

The beauty of the rainbow can be enhanced or marred depending on the situation that creates it. Its purpose, then, is also connected in message and meaning to the situation that creates it.

Your rainbow has a reason. And that reason or purpose is connected to what creates your rainbow.

By now you know that your rainbow, the symbolism for your perspective, attitude and behavior, was initially created by programs you did not choose. Your purpose in life was driven by the attempt to fulfill those programs and give you a sense of security and acceptance. But now you are free. Now you are in control of your programs. You have a different set of perspectives, behaviors and attitudes. You have a different rainbow shining. It follows, then, that you can create the reason for your rainbow. This is what we mean by living life *with purpose.*

Living life freely refers to not having anything in control of you and not carrying any baggage. Living life on purpose means you are making choices about all aspects of your life. Living life *with purpose* means you know why you exist, what your reason is for living. A purpose is often others-centered; it is service oriented and is lived out in all aspects of your life. We know of one person whose purpose is to experience and create joy in all she does. Every aspect of her personal and professional life has this component embedded in it.

Another friend of ours has the purpose of connectivity. She now has the ability and enjoys connecting concepts, people, opportunities, and resources. At work, her purpose serves others in financial ways by connecting people who need services and products with people who have them. In her personal life, people reap great benefit out of her purpose as she connects people with people for compatible benefit. And she does all this naturally and extremely well—all the while causing her to feel deeply fulfilled.

One more friend of ours has the purpose of teaching. Everyone he is engaged with, from his children and their homework to his employees and their projects, find him patient and informative. He always enjoys and is successful at teaching, even difficult subjects or concepts.

Our purpose is to make a positive difference in other people's lives. Whenever we help a business or a person, they reap measurable benefit. All that we study, all that we do, every tool and technique we use or create is designed to make a positive difference in people's lives. When we see our rainbow shine, it is doing so from this purpose.

What is your purpose? You may not know right now, and that's okay. Typically, a purpose is found rather than created. Take a look at your life and find out what your passions are, what you are naturally good at. Notice what you have done naturally in every activity and/or career you have been a part of.

When I, Joann, am coaching, I have my clients look back on their life. I ask them to look at everything they have done naturally, almost automatically, that is others-centered and gives them a sense of fulfillment.

Asking others to give you honest input about what flows from you naturally that serves or benefits others is another way to gather information that can lead you to finding your purpose. Sometimes I have asked my coaching clients to ask people in their past—a teacher, a friend, or a minister, someone who has known them well—to give their perspective. It has been insightful and helpful.

In any case, once you find your purpose, live it. Have it be a part of all that you do. It is the most fulfilling way to live life. Certainly, living life freely on purpose is wonderful. But adding to that the dimension of living live with purpose is incredible. It energizes you; it motivates you, and it can keep you focused. It helps you with prioritization and decision. It gives you reason for living that creates a happiness and peace that goes beyond the first two components of freedom and choice.

But now that you have learned to live your life freely, on purpose, with purpose, we want to tell you something about your rainbow.

It isn't real.

That's right, your rainbow isn't real. It is simply a beautiful illusion that creates your reaction or response.

Your initial programs created your first rainbow—how you looked at the world, and that rainbow had power. It caused you to have a certain set of perspectives, behaviors and interactions. But that rainbow wasn't real. It was only an illusion.

So you learned to get in control of your programs and to reprogram some. You learned to create a different set of perspectives, behaviors and interactions—a new rainbow. But that rainbow isn't real either. It is a beautiful illusion, a familiar illusion, but it is *your* illusion.

There are at least two benefits to understanding this point. First, if the rainbow isn't real but it causes certain responses based on how it shines, then you can see it for what it is and choose your responses. In other words, your rainbow can cease having power over you. Instead, you can have power over it. Your rainbow can shine from your choices. You can enjoy its beauty as it reflects your freedom.

The second benefit regards how you look at other people. When you understand the principles in this book, you become more accepting of other people's behaviors and attitudes. You come to understand that their rainbow is shining from their programs—most of which they didn't choose. When you understand this, you become more understanding and tolerant of them. And this understanding can even give you the knowledge and wisdom to accept and help them.

So now you know. You know how your rainbow shines and why it shines. You have made it to the end of the story. We trust you have the peace and freedom we have seen in so many people who have gone through this process of discovery and growth. So, fly free, live, grow, and live some more. And as you attempt to live out the new you and attempt to share these concepts with someone else but find they don't understand it the way you do, don't worry, you know the truth...

No Two People See the Same Rainbow.

If you are interested in attending a Personal Growth Intensive with Bill and Joann Truby or want more information on how attending a PGI will help you understand the real you and give you the freedom and power to change what you don't like:

Visit our website

www.trubyachievementcenter.com

Or contact us at:

Truby Achievement Center

P.O. Box 1440
Mt. Shasta, CA 96067
Phone: 1 (877) 377-3279 voice, fax, pager (toll free)
(530) 926-2328

info@trubyachievementcenter.com

Appendix 1

Meet Bill and Joann Truby

Bill Truby

Bill Truby, *M.A. MFCC,* is a management consultant and educator trained in psychology. Bill's focus is on improving the quality of human fulfillment and performance in organizations. His clients include architectural, engineering and design firms; manufacturing companies, dental and medical offices, hospitals, wineries, insurance companies, schools, health clubs, and various product, service and sales organizations.

Bill's work includes consulting for goal setting, team building, strategic planning, management transition; training in leadership, communications, sales, delegation, motivation, and other organizational skills. His 5- Step Process For Organizational Success ensures success in any organization.

Bill is a popular speaker and workshop leader for the American Society of Landscape Architects, the Professional Services Management Association, the American Society of Association Executives, the Society of Architectural Administrators and the American Institute of Architects.

He has worked extensively throughout the United States as well as Australia, Singapore, Thailand and Hong Kong. Bill has a Master's Degree in Psychology and has been teaching personal, interpersonal and organizational success strategies for over 20 years.

JOANN TRUBY

Joann Truby is an experienced consultant, speaker, trainer, facilitator, and leadership coach. She has been a consultant to scores of businesses helping them become more successful. Her energetic speaking and training sessions not only provide attendees with meaningful, practical and usable information, she also motivates people to put into practice what she is teaching.

Joann has a broad-based perspective as a consultant, which qualifies her to help firms on many fronts. Her background and training enable her to coach success in everyday issues such as wellness, stress management, and time management. She also brings clients the ability to be successful in communication, leadership, conflict management and teamwork.

Joann aptly facilitates a variety of processes, from goal setting to having effective retreats. Her clients include architectural, engineering and related design profession firms; manufacturing companies, dental and medical offices, hospitals, wineries, insurance companies, schools, health clubs, and various product, service and sales organizations.

As a trainer, leader and educator, Joann's experiential and intuitive approach brings the clients of The Truby Achievement Center a powerful dimension of success. Those who experience her genuine, energetic spirit find motivation and a spirit of helpfulness that leads each individual to believe in the benefits of striving for personal success and balance in life—thus creating more personal fulfillment and corporate success.

One of Joann's unique and special talents is the ability to intuitively give input in training sessions. She knows exactly what to say and do to bring a group of people through a difficult spot or get through an impasse. She is a superior leadership coach. Many top leaders have found her training and coaching skills to be the life-changing ingredient that has enabled their growth and success. She has a rich and multi-faceted life experience where she has developed creative leadership skills and an intuitive ability to help individuals reach their fullest potential.

Printed in the United States
74847LV00005B/40-87

9 780972 589741